HOW THE FRENCH WON WATERLOO (OR THINK THEY DID)

Stephen Clarke lives in Paris, where he divides his time between writing and not writing. His first novel, *A Year in the Merde,* originally became a word-of-mouth hit in 2004, and is now published all over the world. Since then he has published five more bestselling *Merde* novels, as well as non-fiction books such as *1000 Years of Annoying the French* and *Dirty Bertie: An English King Made in France.*

Research for Stephen's books has taken him all over France and America. For *How the French Won Waterloo*, he travelled Europe in search of Napoleon's legacy, as well as delving into the history archives of libraries all over the world. He has now returned to present-day Paris, and is doing his best to live the Entente Cordiale.

For further information on Stephen Clarke and his books, you can visit his website: www.stephenclarkewriter.com or follow him on Twitter @SClarkeWriter

STEPHEN CLARKE

HOW THE FRENCH WON WATERLOO (OR THINK THEY DID)

arrow books

1 3 5 7 9 10 8 6 4 2

Arrow Books
20 Vauxhall Bridge Road
London SW1V 2SA

Arrow Books is part of the Penguin Random House group of companies whose
addresses can be found at global.penguinrandomhouse.com.

Penguin
Random House
UK

First published by Century in 2015
First published by Arrow Books in 2016

www.randomhouse.co.uk

A CIP catalogue record for this book is available from the British Library.

ISBN 9780099594987
ISBN 9780099594994 (Export)

Typeset in Ehrhardt by Palimpsest Book Production Limited,
Falkirk, Stirlingshire
Printed and bound by Clays Ltd, St Ives plc

Penguin Random House is committed to a sustainable future for our business,
our readers and our planet. This book is made from Forest Stewardship Council®
certified paper.

MIX
Paper from
responsible sources
FSC
www.fsc.org   FSC® C018179

To everyone who makes my books possible –
with their thoughts, words, deeds and cups of coffee.

Contents

'It wasn't Lord Wellington who won; his defence was stubborn, and admirably energetic, but he was pushed back and beaten.'

– Captain Marie Jean Baptiste Lemonnier-Delafosse,
French veteran of Waterloo, in his *Souvenirs Militaires*

'This defeat shines with the aura of victory.'

– France's former Prime Minister Dominique
de Villepin, in a recent book about Napoleon

'John Bull was beat at Waterloo!
They'll swear to that in France.'

– Winthrop Mackworth Praed (1802–39),
British politician and poet

INTRODUCTION

'L'histoire est une suite de mensonges sur lesquels on est
d'accord.'

'History is a series of lies about which we agree.'

– Napoleon Bonaparte

Everyone knows who lost the Battle of Waterloo. It was
Napoleon Bonaparte, Emperor of France. Even the French
have to admit that on the evening of 18 June 1815 it was the
Corsican with one hand in his waistcoat who fled the battlefield, his *Grande Armée* in tatters and his reign effectively at
a humiliating end. Napoleon had gambled everything on one
great confrontation with his enemies, and he had lost. The
word 'lost', in this case, having its usual meaning of 'not won',
'been defeated, trounced, hammered', etc.

No one seriously disputes this historical fact. Well, *almost
no one* . . .

Let's look at a few quotations.

'This defeat shines with the aura of victory,' writes France's former Prime Minister Dominique de Villepin in a recent book about Napoleon.

'For the English, Waterloo was a defeat that they won,' claims French historian Jean-Claude Damamme in his study of the battle, published in 1999.

A nineteenth-century French poet called Edouard d'Escola pre-empted this modern doublethink in a poem about Waterloo, prefacing it with a quotation to the effect that 'Defeats are only victories to which fortune has refused to give wings.'

Astonishingly, it is obvious that in some French eyes, where Napoleon is concerned, losing can actually mean winning, or at least not really losing. This despite the fact that after the Battle of Waterloo, Napoleon was ousted from power, forced to flee his country, and then banished into exile on a wind-blown British island for the rest of his life. The only victory parades in France in the summer of 1815 were those by British, Prussian, Austrian and Russian troops as they marched along the Champs-Elysées, past Napoleon's half-built, and rather prematurely named, Arc de Triomphe.

And yet today, visitors to Waterloo, just south of Brussels, might be forgiven for thinking that the result of the battle had been overturned after a stewards' inquiry, and victory handed to the losers. The most spectacular memorial there is the Panorama, a circular building that houses a dramatic 110-metre-long painting of the battle at its height. It is a wonderful picture. You can almost hear the sabres rattling, the cannons firing, the horses snorting, the roars and screams of the fighting men. But there is something very strange about it: Napoleon is in the distance, calmly watching the action, while Wellington seems to be trapped in a corner by a thundering cavalry charge, in imminent danger of having his famous hooked nose hacked off by a French blade. Can this really be the painting that is meant to serve as an official memorial of the battle?

The answer is yes – or rather *oui*, because the painter, Louis Dumoulin, was a Parisian brought in by the Belgians just over a hundred years ago to commemorate the centenary of the most famous historical event that ever took place in their country (apart, perhaps, from the invention of the waffle). This French cavalry charge was the image Dumoulin selected as being representative of the battle as a whole. Napoleon himself could not have chosen a more Bonapartist scene, and yet it was approved by the Belgians. Needless to say, Waterloo is in Wallonie, the French-speaking half of Belgium, where Napoleon has always been hailed as a liberating hero.

Similarly, in the old Waterloo museum next to the Panorama, visitors hoping to watch a (French-made) film about the battle enter the video room beneath a portrait of a defiant-looking general. No, not one of the victors – it's Napoleon again.

A huge new museum is currently being built at Waterloo in readiness for the bicentenary. It will probably give a more balanced, and historically accurate, view of the battle. But one thing seems certain: the new gift shop will be just like the old one – that is, selling ten times more souvenir statuettes, medals and portraits of Napoleon than of anyone else involved in the battle. French revisionists seem to have taken possession of Waterloo, and Napoleon's image is everywhere. He has been turned into the icon that represents the events of 18 June 1815. He lost, but it doesn't seem to matter.

It is a beautifully French contradiction that provokes two main questions: Who exactly is behind this rewriting of history that has been going on ever since the battle ended? And why do they feel the need to indulge in such outrageous denial?

Luckily for me (and, I hope, for you, dear reader), the answers are fascinatingly complex. But let me give a brief introductory summary before going into much more detail in the book.

First of all, Napoleon has an army of fiercely loyal fans. They have been around since he was Emperor of France, and they are as fanatical today as they ever were. These are the people who dress up in Napoleonic uniform and shout 'Vive l'Empereur!' at battle re-enactments, who give generous grants to Napoleonic research (as long as the thesis flatters Napoleon), and who paid 1.8 million euros for one of his famous black hats when it came up for auction in November 2014.

Among these fans is a belligerent battalion of French historians who refuse to associate Napoleon's name with anything as shameful as defeat. To achieve this feat of historical acrobatics, they will use any argument they can muster: at Waterloo, they contend, Napoleon might have lost to Blücher but he beat Wellington; the British cheated by choosing the battlefield; Napoleon's generals disobeyed him;

traitors revealed his plans; the French government prevented him from mustering another army and fighting on; etc., etc. Anything to have Napoleon emerge as a winner of some sort.

In any case, these fan-historians constantly remind us, Napoleon was France's greatest ever champion: he won far more battles than he lost, and during his short reign France was at the peak of its influence in the world, with most of continental Europe under the Napoleonic yoke. To these determined and highly outspoken Bonapartists, Waterloo is nothing more than a minor blemish on Napoleon's glorious record.

And in a way, the whole of modern French history revolves around, or has its roots in, Napoleon. Even historians who see him as a dictator and are relieved that his imperial regime was toppled will readily acknowledge Napoleon's greatness and the undeniable influence he exerts on present-day life in France. After all, most of the laws he drafted are still in place (minus a few of his more sexist clauses); he invented France's education system; and all modern French presidents model themselves on his autocratic style of leadership – they even live and work in his former palace, surrounded by his furniture.

Which brings us to the question of why exactly all these people are in denial about Waterloo, the battle that – like it or not – ended Napoleon's political and military career. Is it a classic emotional blockage, patriotism gone mad, or is there something even more subtly French at play?

Well, yes to all those rhetorical questions; but the central reason seems to be that, ever since 1815, it has been vital for the French national psyche to see Napoleon as a winner.

If he is a loser, so is France. And if there is one thing the French as a nation hate, it is losing – especially to *les Anglais*.

This is why even those French people who acknowledge (at least partial) defeat at Waterloo are determined to extract some form of triumph from the debacle: they will say that the outnumbered French troops were defending the nobler cause, that their glorious defiance made them the tragic heroes of the day, and so on. There is no end to the evasive action they will take.

To illustrate all this historical escapology, I have concentrated mainly on French sources – Waterloo veterans, nineteenth-century French novelists and poets who experienced Napoleon's regime, French historians writing from 1815 right up to today, and of course Napoleon himself, who had time while in exile to relive (and rewrite) every second of the battle.

Exploring their original words and impressions has given me a vivid insight into what the French have been saying about their beloved *Empereur* for the last two centuries, and what they're still doing to defend his iconic image.

English-language commentators seem to spend a lot of time reworking the old argument that Waterloo was purely and simply a hard-won Anglo-Prussian victory that got rid of Napoleon and changed the course of European history.

But Napoleon's admirers, past and present, show that the Battle of Waterloo and its 200-year-long aftermath have been a lot more complicated – and a lot more French – than that.

Stephen Clarke, Paris, February 2015

PART ONE

1

~

NAPOLEON WAS A PEACE-LOVER

'La paix est le vœu de mon cœur, mais la guerre n'a jamais
été contraire à ma gloire.'
'My heart wishes for peace, but war has never diminished my
glory.'

– Napoleon Bonaparte, in a letter to England's
King George III in 1805

I

First, the context. Why exactly did Napoleon Bonaparte
confront the Duke of Wellington and Prussia's Generalfeldmarschall Gebhard Blücher at a crossroads in Belgium on
that rainy day of 18 June 1815 – aside from the fact that
Belgium was conveniently central for all three?

The main reason is, of course, that Britain and France
had been at war virtually non-stop since 1337. The
Napoleonic Wars were more or less a continuation of the

medieval Hundred Years War, and in 1815, things had come to an ugly head. As the nineteenth-century French historian Jules Michelet, author of a nineteen-volume *Histoire de France*, put it: 'The war of wars, the combat of combats, is England against France; all the rest are mere episodes.'*

French Bonapartists insist that Napoleon didn't want war with Britain. Napoleon himself said so. He was a peace-loving man, much more interested in modernising his own country than firing cannons at his neighbours. All he wanted to do was write new laws, create new schools, and turn beetroot into sugar (all of which he actually did, as we shall see in a later chapter).

The Prussian ambassador to France – not a man instinctively favourable towards the French – confirmed this as early as 1802. Marquis Girolamo Lucchesini (he was an Italian in the service of Friedrich Wilhelm III of Prussia) reported to Berlin that Napoleon was talking convincingly of 'canals to complete or dig, roads to repair or build, ports to clean out, cities to embellish, religious institutions to found, and educational resources to pay for'. According to the Prussian-Italian diplomat, Napoleon wanted to 'devote money to agriculture, industry, business and arts that would otherwise be absorbed and exhausted by war'. In the circumstances, it was impossible, surely, to imagine a single French franc getting spent on cannons, muskets and cavalry helmets?

A more cynical diplomat might have asked this peace-loving

---

* All quotations from French sources are my own. Though I have tried to be scrupulously objective when translating, *naturellement*.

version of Napoleon why, after seizing power in France with a military coup in 1799, he had continued the war against Britain and its allies the Austrians, Italians and Russians, or why he had invaded Italy in 1800, confirmed the annexation of Belgium, and maintained a puppet pro-French regime in Holland.

Napoleon would have replied – with some justification – that he had just been finishing off what was started during the French Revolution, before he even came along. He had simply fought a few battles, discouraged the country's enemies from invading, consolidated his position as leader of France, and built a platform from which he could oversee his grand peacetime plan for the nation. Put like that, it sounds convincing, and the Prussian ambassador clearly believed it.

So too does modern French historian Jean-Claude Damamme, one of Napoleon's most fervent defenders. He blames Britain (or 'England' as he calls it, like any Frenchman with an anti-British axe to grind) for the Napoleonic Wars. France, he says, was too dangerous a competitor, 'a threat to the ascendancy that England has always considered a divine right'. With France united behind their glamorous young leader, Monsieur Damamme asserts, it became obvious to the Brits that their only hope of European domination was to eliminate him.

Damamme even accuses the English of being behind the so-called 'attentat de la rue Saint-Nicaise' (the rue Saint-Nicaise attack) when, on Christmas Eve, 1800, a wine barrel packed with explosives was ignited as Napoleon's carriage drove past, demolishing forty-six houses, killing twenty-two people and injuring around a hundred, but leaving Napoleon miraculously unscathed.

The Emperor had been on his way to the theatre with his wife Josephine to see Haydn's *Creation*, and had fallen asleep in the carriage. The explosion not only woke Napoleon up, it also aroused a fierce desire for vengeance. He had a group of 'conspirators' executed despite evidence proving that they were innocent, before begrudgingly accepting that the true guilty parties were royalists who wanted to restore the monarchy. Jean-Claude Damamme, though, blames the British, whom he accuses of stirring up virtually all the anti-Napoleonic unrest on the continent over the next fifteen years, and paying the Belgians, Dutch and Prussians to turn against the French (an accusation that was largely justified, as we will see).

Faced with this endless British troublemaking, Napoleon was, in Bonapartist French eyes, like a kung fu master, meditating peacefully on his prayer mat about progress and democracy while a gang of irritating English boys threw acorns at him, finally forcing him to get up and give them a slap.

This theory is confirmed (again, in French eyes) by King George III's sudden unprovoked blockade of France's ports in May 1803. Despite this English aggression, the French contend that Napoleon continued to push for peace, and quote an eloquent letter to George III on 2 January 1805, in which Napoleon says that 'my first sentiment is a wish for peace' and that 'reason is powerful enough for us to find a way to reconcile all our differences'.

However, a closer look at the missive – part peace offering, part (self-)love letter – reveals that it is more a case of 'come and have a go if you think you're hard enough'. Napoleon informs the hereditary English King that he (Napoleon) was 'called to the throne of France by providence and by the vote of the Senate, the people and the army' – which surely outweighs a mere accident of birth. Napoleon then declares that 'my heart wishes for peace, but war has never diminished my glory'. He reminds King George and his government that 'I have proved to the world, I think, that I fear none of the uncertainties of war' and that a conflict between Britain and France would be 'pointless, and [a British] victory cannot be assumed'. As for expansionism, Napoleon innocently asks the King of England whether he doesn't think he has enough colonies already – 'more than you can hope to keep'. It is a threat more thinly veiled than one of Josephine's famously transparent dresses.

Napoleon ends his letter by asserting generously that 'the world is big enough for both of our nations to live in'. But King George and his Prime Minister William Pitt the Younger obviously didn't agree, because they never even bothered to reply.

Not that the French Emperor was completely without friends in Britain at the time. James Fox, the leader of the opposition, was a virulent anti-royalist who had supported the French Revolution, and his pacifist group in the British parliament numbered about twenty-five MPs. War with France, Fox said, 'is entirely the fault of our Ministers and not of Bonaparte'. Though, typically for a politician, this support was largely based on self-interest: Fox was hoping that William Pitt's anti-French lobbying would fail, so that Pitt himself would have to resign. In truth, Fox wasn't that big a Bonaparte fan. He visited Napoleon in 1803 and apparently spent most of their meeting haranguing the Frenchman about freedom of speech and censorship of the press.

Meanwhile, Napoleon had received a warning from the Russian ambassador to London that Britain's aim would 'always be to destroy France and then reign despotically over the whole universe'. (Actually, apart from the 'despotically', most Brits of the time would have agreed wholeheartedly.)

Faced with this belligerence, so the French argument goes, the peace-loving Napoleon had no option but a return to war against France's traditional enemy, Britain. As he expressed it in his memoirs: 'I had more reason than most to make peace, and if I didn't do so, it is obviously because I wasn't able to.'

But for a man who seems to be saying 'bof, OK, let's fight, if you really want to', in 1805 Bonaparte threw himself into war with a startling amount of enthusiasm.

II

In fact, Napoleon loved a good battle. He had been trained as a soldier since childhood, having been sent from his native Corsica to a military academy in mainland France at the age of nine. There, legend has it, he commanded his classmates in a successful snowball fight.* At fifteen, he entered Paris's elite Ecole Militaire where, no doubt because of his skill with snowballs, he specialised in artillery warfare. In short, here was a man who had been learning how to fight professionally all his life, and who had chosen to specialise in the branch of war that involves the loudest explosions and the most collateral damage. A Buddhist he was not.

Napoleon first came to prominence in the French army in 1793 by commanding an attack on a British fleet stationed in Toulon, in the south of France, a city that had rebelled against the Revolution. Erecting artillery batteries and accurately bombarding vulnerable sections of the city wall and the British ships, he had effectively retaken Toulon, and been made a general at the tender age of twenty-four. In 1795, he was then instrumental in suppressing a royalist revolt in Paris, blasting the armed crowds surrounding the parliament building with point-blank cannon fire for some forty-five minutes. Then in 1799 he seized power by invading the French parliament with a group of bayonet-waving soldiers. In short, Napoleon's favourite political tools were hot lead and cold steel.

He also felt most at home when on military campaigns. Out in the field with his troops he was in his element, engrossed in logistical problems, which fascinated him. One

---

* That is no joke – the snowball story really is told in French biographies, as is the tale about young Napoleon 'annexing' other pupils' vegetable patches in the school gardens. His whole life is treated by his French admirers as the stuff of heroic legend.

of his life's greatest works was a total reorganisation and modernisation of the French army, dividing it into self-sufficient units of around 25,000 men, each with its own marshal or general in command of a body of infantry supported by cavalry and, of course, a large contingent of artillery. These units were designed to be fast-moving (it was not uncommon for inexperienced footsoldiers to die of exhaustion during long marches), and during a major campaign they were under orders to stay within 30 kilo-metres or so (a day's march) of each other, so that Napoleon could bring them into action quickly when an enemy was engaged. The reorganisation went deep, right down to the small sections of half a dozen men who formed teams within their larger battalion. Napoleon was obsessive about detail, and the army was where he expressed this obsession with all his fiery-yet-bureaucratic Franco-Corsican temperament.

At the heart of the action, commanding his hundreds of thousands of loyal men, shaping the destiny of nations with his carefully aimed cannon fire, Napoleon felt completely at home, not least because his campaign bivouac was more luxurious than the VIP tent at the Glastonbury festival. Here, his gift for planning was at its most ingenious.

An exhibition staged in 2014 in Corsica, 'Le Bivouac de Napoléon', included a picturesque blue-and-white marquee that wouldn't look out of place as the tea tent at a modern royal garden party, and a camp bed equipped with a thick mattress and enveloped in a green silk tasselled curtain. His folding leather chair was a more comfortable version of the kind we see Steven Spielberg sitting in for marathon directing sessions, while the panther-patterned carpet looked like something out of a 1980s pop video.

France's most famous furniture designers, potters, cutlery-makers and metal-workers were commissioned to create monogrammed crockery, a full range of easily folding chairs, desks, tables and footstools, dismountable candlesticks, a mobile brazier and even a folding bidet (which sounds rather dangerous) – all of it made of 'noble' materials like silver, gold-plated bronze, crystal, fine porcelain, silk and walnut. This nomad's palace would travel with Napoleon in a small convoy of carriages so that he could live on the road in luxury for months on end. He was the nineteenth-century equivalent of a rock star on tour.

And like those rock stars, he was determined to export the music of his cannons to as many territories as possible. Between 1804 (when he declared himself Emperor of France, as opposed to a mere 'consul') and 1811, Napoleon battled his way across Europe, annexing Switzerland, Italy, Spain, Austria, Slovenia, Croatia, Poland and most of modern-day Germany.

Incidentally, by taking over several German princedoms and imposing his brother Jérôme as King of Westphalia in 1807, Napoleon accidentally did the world a great favour. The Grimm brothers, Jacob and Wilhelm, had just finished studying law and were about to embark on a legal career, but when the French occupiers imposed Napoleon's new 'Code' (of which more in Chapter 8) the brothers found it much too rigid compared with ancient German traditions, and decided to devote their lives to collecting folk tales instead. Westphalian law's loss was the world's (and especially Walt Disney's) gain.

Wanting to spread his influence beyond the borders of his empire, Napoleon also imposed an embargo against trading with Britain on countries that he hadn't occupied, like Russia and the whole of Scandinavia.* As France's former Prime Minister Dominique Villepin expresses it in one of his history books, Napoleon had 'a dream of France that was bigger than the French'. Put less patriotically, Napoleon wanted all of Europe to bow before him as its emperor, and very nearly succeeded in getting them all on their knees.

III

There was one rival who, despite all Napoleon's protests of peace, he *really* wanted to beat. That was, of course, Britain, whom he (quite rightly) blamed for all the European mischief-making against him. The British proudly and openly invested in beating Napoleon, distributing money and munitions to anyone who was willing to oppose the French. It has been estimated that Britain spent £1.5 billion on fighting Napoleon – an unimaginable fortune in the early 1800s – half of which was borrowed. Britain's anti-Napoleonic debt was so huge that it was only paid off in 1906.

* Napoleon called his embargo the Blocus Continental, which probably goes some way to explaining the traditional feeling among Brits of being separate from 'the continent'. British 'splendid isolation' comes in part from Napoleon's desire to isolate it.

The Brits naturally alleged that this was all for the good of world peace. George Canning, Foreign Secretary between 1807 and 1809, once said that 'Whenever the true balance of the world comes to be adjusted, it is only through us alone that they can look for secure and effectual tranquillity.' (Britain was never known for its humility, least of all in the nineteenth century.) Until then, Mr Canning said, Britain could justifiably cause trouble wherever it wanted: 'Until there can be a final settlement that shall last, everything should remain as unsettled as possible.' This was a principle that applied especially to France, the traditional enemy.

True to his principles of cannonball diplomacy, Napoleon therefore spent much of 1803, 1804 and 1805 planning a mass invasion of the south coast of England via hot-air balloon, giant barges and even a tunnel. Sadly for him, the scheme sank without trace when Nelson smashed the French fleet at Trafalgar in October 1805 – a victory that cemented Britannia's rule over the waves and ensured that the *Grande Armée*'s trip across the Channel would get very choppy indeed.

Napoleon duly changed tack, and decided that the way to hurt Britain was to aim for its soft, sweet underbelly – India, the source of its tea, spices and cheap cotton goods, the pride of its empire. George III had already lost America (with French help), and the loss of India would therefore be a doubly painful blow.

There was something of an Alexander the Great fantasy in Napoleon's plan to march through Turkey and right across north-western Asia. And Napoleon knew that he would need

Russia's blessing and logistical help, so in March 1808, the French Emperor wrote to Czar Alexander I outlining his ambitious scheme. 'Everything can be signed before March 15,' Napoleon enthused. 'By May 1 our troops will be in Asia . . . The English, threatened in India, expelled from the Middle East, will be crushed beneath the weight of events.'

Predictably, the conquest of Asia didn't go ahead that quickly, and a meeting between Napoleon and the Czar was arranged for September in Erfurt, Germany, which Napoleon had recently seized from the Prussians. He hoped to use the so-called 'Entrevue d'Erfurt' (the word *entrevue* making it sound slightly like a job interview) to dazzle the Russian Czar with his power and vision, and invited along all the crowned heads of France's puppet European states. Napoleon also took the entire national theatre company, the Comédie Française, with him to perform the greatest works of French literature (most of which were recycled Greek and Roman tragedies, presumably intended to depress Czar Alexander into acquiescence). He even made a tentative offer to cement the alliance by marrying Czar Alexander's sister Catherine.

Napoleon was therefore disappointed to come home from the two-week-long series of talks and theatre evenings with nothing more than a tame Franco-Russian treaty asking Britain to recognise France's claim to Spain and Russia's recent occupation of Finland and Sweden. No Russian wife, and no Russian promise to support an attack on India.

Napoleon couldn't understand why Alexander had been 'difficult' during the talks. What had gone wrong?

Well, predictably, it was a Frenchman who had scuppered

Napoleon's grand plan – Charles-Maurice de Talleyrand-Périgord (Talleyrand for short). He was France's own Minister of Foreign Affairs, and had become disenchanted with Napoleon's habit of dealing with foreign affairs himself – with cannons rather than witticisms, for which Talleyrand was famed.

At Erfurt, Talleyrand held secret talks with Czar Alexander, and apparently lectured the Russian on the folly of allying with Napoleon. 'What are you doing here?' he is said to have asked Alexander. 'It is up to you to save Europe, and you will only do that if you stand up to Napoleon. The people of France are civilised, their sovereign is not. The sovereign of Russia is civilised, his people are not. It is therefore up to the sovereign of Russia to ally with the people of France.'

When Napoleon found out about all this, he convened a meeting of his advisers at which he publicly called Talleyrand 'de la merde dans des bas de soie', or 'shit in silk stockings'. Why he didn't have him executed or at least exiled is a mystery. Other anti-Bonaparte plotters went to the scaffold on the strength of a whim or a rumour. But Talleyrand miraculously survived five French regimes while heads were falling all around him, and would later play a key role in sealing Napoleon's fate after Waterloo.

For the moment, though, the treacherous Talleyrand had merely demolished Napoleon's great scheme to invade India and humiliate Britain, and had thereby virtually assured the war with Russia that would decimate his Emperor's beloved *Grande Armée*. It was a good start.

Talleyrand's machinations were also typical of the French

back-stabbing that, according to Bonapartists, would eventually lead to Napoleon's demise. As we shall see, the higher Napoleon climbed, the greater the danger that a traitor or a coward would bring him crashing down. Partly this was because his most faithful companions were courageous generals who would fall in battle, forcing him to appoint less reliable aides (an excuse frequently used to defend Napoleon against charges of being a bad judge of character). But most of all, Bonapartist historians are keen to stress that Napoleon was a man with a unique greatness that was bound to arouse envy among his contemporaries, even his fellow Frenchmen; that his vision was so all-encompassing that it was impossible for mere mortals to comprehend; and, most importantly, that anything that went wrong was almost certainly someone else's fault. Nothing must be blamed on the great *Empereur*.

IV

Sadly for Napoleon, his defeats have left an indelible trace on the French language. One of these linguistic black marks is the saying (still used today) 'c'est la Bérézina', meaning that a situation is total chaos, and that everything is about to go horribly wrong. In the kitchen before a big French family dinner, if the veal comes out of the oven overcooked, the potatoes aren't ready, the wine is too warm, and a cherubic child is found decorating the walls with the chocolate mousse, 'c'est la Bérézina'.

It's a saying inspired by a great national tragedy that took place between 25 and 27 November 1812 at the River Berezina, when the frost-bitten, starved remnants of Napoleon's *Grande Armée* made a frantic attempt to squeeze across two hastily improvised bridges and escape from Russia. Out of 80,000 or so men who had managed to tramp 640 kilometres westwards across the frozen steppes from Moscow, only 35,000 made it.

And yet, predictably, Napoleon's French fans hail it as a victory. The historian Jean Tulard, who started writing books about Napoleon in the 1960s and hasn't stopped yet, calls Berezina 'a French victory in difficult conditions . . . Napoleon and a large part of his troops escaped'. The whole thing was, if you like, a sort of Dunkirk.

But surely any comparisons with 1940 are absurd. Admittedly, Dunkirk was a retreat, also 'in difficult conditions', but it was a tactical withdrawal that boosted national morale and prevented an invasion of England by the Nazis. Berezina was a dash for safety by the half-dead survivors of the largest army Europe had ever seen, and ultimately led to Napoleon's first abdication. It was like saving a few family photos from a blazing house. Though to the most fervent Bonapartists, only one photo was important.

And it had all started out so promisingly. In June 1812, with an empire stretching from south-west Spain up to north-eastern Poland, from Holland down to the toe of Italy, Napoleon decided that he was not going to take any nonsense from the 'difficult' Czar who had begun to defy his *Blocus Continental*. Buying coffee, tea, sugar and cotton (products of the perfidious British Empire), and cheap knives, scissors and machines (the result of Britain's dizzying technological progress), was a Russian slap in the face to French superiority. Wasn't Napoleon's empire capable of supplying everything that Europe needed? Well, no, it clearly wasn't, and the Russians were rubbing his nose in the fact.

Napoleon therefore launched the grandest military operation Europe had ever seen. Figures vary widely, but most historians agree that more than half a million soldiers began to cross the Polish border into Russia on 24 June 1812. About three-quarters of them were French, the rest coming from right across Napoleon's empire – there were Italians, Belarusians, Austrians, Swiss, Lithuanians, Poles, Danes, Spaniards, Bavarians, Prussians, and even an Irish brigade. Napoleon himself told his memoirist Emmanuel de Las Cases that he had 400,000 men with 240,000 in reserve. Opposing them were around 400,000 Russians, including a large proportion of hastily conscripted, underpaid serfs, bolstered by 80,000 of the scariest soldiers on the continent, the Cossacks.

As the *Grande Armée* set off towards Moscow, the sun glinting brightly on their breastplates and bayonets, Napoleon must have felt sure that victory would soon be his. He knew that the main Russian army was not far off – it was just a matter of catching up and destroying it. In his *Napoléon: l'Immortel de Sainte-Hélène*, the final part of a four-volume biography, the French historian Max Gallo imagines the Emperor bursting with a mixture of pride and impatience as he gazed out over the scene through his looking glass. 'The hills and valleys were full of men, horses and wagons. The weapons were shining beneath the incandescent sky . . . What an army! He [Napoleon] slapped his boots with his riding whip, strode back and forth humming "Malbrough [*sic*] s'en va-t-en guerre".* Who could resist such power in motion?' This huge French army was accompanied by 30,000 carts carrying two million bottles of brandy and 28 million bottles of wine, mobile *boulangeries* and several tons of wheat, blacksmiths' equipment, ammunition, medicine, and of course officers' picnic sets. There was also a whole column of cattle – a regiment of steak tartare on the hoof. Napoleon himself travelled in a sort of horse-drawn camper van, with a desk and enough room for strategy meetings.

Speed was of the essence, so it was quick march all the way for the footsoldiers. And very soon they began to die – of typhus and dysentery from infected water, of heat exhaustion and, despite all the wheat and beef, of hunger.

The reason for these early and unexpected French casualties was that the Russians had begun to play Napoleon at his own game of tactical warfare. What started out as a genuine attempt to avoid a pitched battle for fear of losing the war evolved into a strategy to draw the French deeper and deeper into Russia, stretching their supply lines and allowing the feared Cossacks to pick off isolated units. Apart from one major battle at Borodino on 7 September (the bloodiest day of the whole Napoleonic Wars, resulting in around 40,000 dead, wounded or captured *on each side*) the Russians avoided

---

* 'Marlborough goes off to war'. Ironically, Napoleon is depicted humming an old French song, sung to the tune of 'For He's a Jolly Good Fellow', about the Duke of Marlborough's campaigns against Louis XIV. Or perhaps it was not ironic – it might have been a way of implying that Napoleon was a greater general than the famous Englishman.

direct confrontation.* The retreating Russian army also practised a tactic that at first confused and then began to exasperate
the French. Every town that the *Grande Armée* reached had
been systematically emptied of its food supplies and burned
to the ground. Napoleon might have contended that an army
marches on its stomach, but his rapidly advancing men had
no way to replenish their larders.

Napoleon entered Moscow itself in mid-September
proclaiming victory and expecting a delegation from the
Czar accepting defeat. In the event he found no one except
a few Muscovites who had preferred not to abandon their
homes. Any remaining sense of victory was dispelled when,
at a secret signal, the city was set ablaze. Napoleon recalled
his dismay at seeing 'mountains of swirling red flames, like
huge ocean waves, exploding up into the sky of fire, then
sinking into the sea of flames below'.

The fires burned for a week, destroying 90 per cent of
Moscow's buildings.** To the French it was unthinkable –

* The French won at Borodino, and prefer the battle to be called Moskowa
– Napoleon gave his Marshal Ney the title 'Prince de la Moskowa' for
his gallantry there. But for once, the rule that the victor names the battle
doesn't apply, and everyone outside France refers to the Battle of Borodino.
Proof, perhaps, of the extent of Napoleon's overall defeat in Russia.
** Incidentally, the governor of Moscow who emptied the city of food and
burned it down was a man called Fiodor Rostoptchine. Rich Muscovites
were so furious with him that he was forced into exile, eventually ending
up in France in 1817 (which by then was under a new, anti-Bonapartist
regime). There, Fiodor's daughter Sofia married the nephew of a general
who had been with Napoleon at Moscow, and she became one of France's
most famous children's writers under the name La Comtesse de Ségur.

they would never have burned their beloved Paris, even to save their country. But of course Czar Alexander didn't really care about Moscow – he was safely installed in his palace 700 kilometres away in St Petersburg.

'If Moscow hadn't been set on fire,' Napoleon later confided to his memoirist Emmanuel de Las Cases, 'Czar Alexander would have been forced to sue for peace.' The obvious problem was that it *had* been set on fire. So, faced with the prospect of living through a Russian winter with nowhere to bivouac except charred ruins, and with meagre supplies for his men and horses, Napoleon had no choice but to start marching back in the opposite direction.

The *Empereur* dictated to Las Cases that 'the march from Moscow cannot be called a retreat, because the army was victorious'. But as soon as he left Moscow in mid-October, the flanks and the rear of his 'victorious' yet back-tracking army began to be harassed by Russians who picked off whole units of demoralised Frenchmen. With no grass and no fodder, the *Grande Armée*'s horses started to die. Those that could still stand were slaughtered and eaten. So the cavalry became infantry, the artillery had to abandon its horse-drawn cannons, and all the remaining supply wagons were left by the roadside. In early November, winter set in with a vengeance, and had a perverse effect: the extreme cold caused all the tin buttons on the *Grande Armée*'s uniforms to crumble into dust. Now the men couldn't even button up their coats to shut out the biting wind.

'If the great freeze hadn't set in two weeks earlier than usual, the army would have made it to Smolensk intact,'

Napoleon told Las Cases. 'We had reason to believe, judging by the temperature records of the previous 20 years, that the thermometer would not drop below freezing in November.' (Like all defeated generals, Napoleon was highly skilled at hindsight and if onlys.)

Of the huge army that had crossed into Russia in June, about 200,000 men died there. Napoleon also suffered the loss of around 180,000 prisoners, as well as almost 200,000 deserters who drifted away during the retreat, some of whom were lucky enough to find an unlikely welcome among the Russians. Only 30,000 men made it back to France. It was, as the French say, 'la Bérézina'.

In short, even if Napoleon liked to remember his over-ambitious excursion into Russia as a *victoire*, the result of the campaign was that three years later, he would fight at Waterloo with an army of new recruits and reservists.

But the most serious consequence for Napoleon himself was even greater – the Russian campaign had proved to his enemies that the great French Emperor was only human after all. He and his *Grande Armée* could be beaten.

V

Arriving back in Paris in a borrowed open carriage (his own had broken an axle after bumping at top speed through Germany), Napoleon was so dirty and unshaven that his servants didn't recognise him until he marched into his wife's bedroom, from which all strange men were banned. Clearly desperate to put a good spin on things, Napoleon's aides broadcast the news to the people that the Emperor had covered the 1,000 kilometres from Dresden in only four days. In other words, he had broken the world retreating record, *vive l'Empereur*.

True to form, Talleyrand was informing everyone in Paris that this was 'le commencement de la fin' – the beginning of the end. But Napoleon, never happier than when planning troop movements on the grand scale, threw his energies into a frantic reorganisation of his armies. He set about raising a new force of over 200,000 recruits to carry on the fight, even paying for uniforms and equipment with his own private gold supply, which was stored in barrels in the basement of the Tuileries Palace.

Faced with revolts in several of his German puppet states, and the defection of Prussia to the Russian camp, Napoleon knew that it was vital to stay on good terms with Austria. This, he thought, would be easy. After all, in 1810 he had divorced his first wife Josephine and married Marie-Louise, the eldest daughter of Emperor Franz I of Austria. They had a baby son, and to flatter Franz, Napoleon had Marie-Louise write frequent letters home informing the Austrian Emperor that the young prince would one day be crowned King (not Emperor) of France, creating a new Franco-Austrian royal dynasty. Marie-Louise, who was twenty-one years younger than her husband, would be regent of France, and she was already nominally Queen of Italy. Even better, Napoleon would build a new royal palace for his son, a gigantic construction on the hill across the Seine from the Ecole Militaire, a royal residence two-thirds the size of

Versailles just on the edge of Paris. What more could the Austrian Emperor ask of his French son-in-law?

Unfortunately for Napoleon, the Viennese court was under the influence of a dispossessed aristocrat: Clemens Metternich, who was still smarting from the loss of his family's immense landholdings on the Rhine, which had been seized by the French in 1794. Metternich was now Austria's Foreign Minister, and relished his revenge, at first promising peace with Napoleon, only to stab him in the back by signing an anti-French treaty with Russia and Prussia. Meanwhile the British had done the same, and diabolically promised a grant of £666,666 to the Prussian army. The European war that would eventually bring about Napoleon's downfall was now inevitable.

VI

As if all these northern developments weren't depressing enough, there was also bad news from the south: Napoleon's brother Joseph (nominally King of Spain) had been taken by surprise while dallying with a mistress, and almost shot by a British cavalryman. Joseph is a prime example of the unreliable links in Napoleon's chain of command who get blamed by Bonapartist historians for allowing disasters to happen. Now Joseph's army was being chased out of Spain by a relatively little-known English general called Wellington, who would eventually invade Napoleon's France and capture Toulouse and Bordeaux, where he would be hailed as a liberator by citizens tired of war.

Napoleon reacted by continuing to build his army, until by the summer of 1813 he had managed to cajole or force 360,000 Frenchmen into uniform. Even so, he began to suffer his first personal defeats of the wars that bore his name. Over three days from 15 to 18 October 1813, Napoleon and his marshals engaged in several pitched battles with the Russians, Prussians, Austrians and Swedes, most notably at Leipzig in Germany. Outnumbered almost two to one there, the French lost about 45,000 dead and wounded and 26,000 prisoners, and were forced to make a dash for France to save themselves.

French historians often divide campaigns into several battles, thereby giving themselves a longer list of victories (as we will see them do in the days preceding and following Waterloo). Here, though, they do the opposite, referring simply to the 'Bataille de Leipzig', presumably so as to limit the number of defeats.

And Bonapartists are quick to point out that if Leipzig was a defeat, it was not one for Napoleon himself. His enemies avoided confronting him directly, preferring to face up to the sections of his army commanded by his marshals. Every time Napoleon rushed into action, his opponents withdrew. He complained that even Blücher fled instead of fighting: 'There was no way of getting at him. I hardly fired one or two shots.' This was an artilleryman's frustration talking.

Not only this, when the enemy had attacked, they had copied Napoleon's tactics, using cannons to smash holes in infantry and cavalry lines before charging into the breach.

Thanks to the Prussians' two-to-one superiority, this was bound to succeed. In a way, Bonapartists can argue, Leipzig was a victory for Napoleonic tactics. Not that the Emperor himself would have gained much solace from this.

Back in Paris, the treacherous Talleyrand, who once said that 'speech was given to man so that he could disguise his thoughts', was making his own thoughts crystal clear. Napoleon was finished, he told everyone. 'He has nothing more to fight with. He is exhausted. He will crawl under his bed and hide.'

Talleyrand's quips were usually bitchy but accurate. (Another of his favourite sayings was: 'Never speak ill of yourself. Your friends will do it for you.' Which in his case was understandably accurate.) In this case, though, he got it very wrong. Napoleon was not a man to crawl under a bed, even if, like the bunk in his campaign bivouac, it was set up on a comfortable panther-pattern carpet. This was not 1940, when the French would throw down their arms almost as soon as a German set foot on French soil – Napoleon's fight to defend his territory was only just beginning.

VII

To the French, the word 'allies' is a double-edged sword. Triple-edged, even. Of course it calls to mind positive thoughts of the Second World War, in which France ended up as one of the victorious allies. But when used about the Napoleonic Wars, *'alliés'* is more of a dirty word. It refers to the nations who ganged up on France and eventually ousted Napoleon from power. The scorn the word evokes is all too clear in Jean-Claude Damamme's book on Waterloo, in which he calls the allied nations of Austria, Russia and Prussia 'a pretty trio of former losers'. Of course he couldn't include one of the major allies, Britain, in his insult because the Brits had not been beaten by Napoleon, and never would be.*

Napoleon's own view of the foreigners threatening his homeland, and his crown, in 1814 is clear from a motivational speech he gave to his Old Guard (not that many of them were old, most of the seasoned campaigners having been left behind in the Russian ice). As they prepared to meet the allied invasion, he told them: 'Soldiers, we are going to chase these secondary foreign princes from our territory. We don't want to meddle with the affairs of foreign countries, but woe betide him who meddles in ours.' Here, he seems to be forgetting his own past incursions into Italy, Spain, Portugal, Belgium, Holland, Germany, Poland and Russia, as well as his plans to invade England and India. Nevertheless, the invaders now began to 'meddle in his affairs' with a vengeance.

The so-called Campagne de France of 1814 is one of the short campaigns the French like to split up into individually named battles, because even though Napoleon ultimately lost the campaign, he did pull off a few victories, despite

---

* The French also refer to the coalition of allies opposing Napoleon as *les coalisés*, which makes them sound rather like a bloodclot.

the fact that his 300,000-odd remaining men were facing a million *alliés*.

At Brienne le Château, for example, 200 kilometres south-east of Paris, Napoleon ousted the Russian and Prussian occupiers from the aforementioned chateau, which must have been a sweet victory for him – Brienne was where he had gone to school when he first left Corsica as a nine-year-old military cadet. The fact that the occupiers pulled out in the night after a battle in which losses were equal on both sides (3,000 each), because they wanted to join up with an even bigger allied army a few kilometres away, is of no consequence. History (French history, anyway) lists Brienne as a Napoleonic victory.

The same goes for another unfamiliar name, la Bataille de Champaubert, fought on 10 February. Here, 90 kilometres north-west of Brienne, around 6,000 French soldiers commanded by Napoleon routed a force of only 4,500 Russians, and captured their general. An almost inconsequential skirmish compared to Napoleon's great victories at Jena, Austerlitz and Wagram, but it merits an avenue Champaubert in Paris, and in the town itself there is a monument dedicated to 'les victoires napoléoniennes du 10 février 1814' – note the plural.

On 12 February, Napoleon again carried off the day, this time at Château-Thierry, though given the low number of casualties ('only' 3,750 out of 50,000 men on the battlefield), by Napoleonic standards it hardly counts as more than a heated argument.

Over the following month, other French victories followed,

at places that are remembered only by the towns concerned (and their tourist offices) – Vauchamps, Mormant, Montereau,* Craonne, Laon. To anyone except a keen Bonapartist, they were all desperate rearguard actions, like a midget slapping the knees of a giant in the boxing ring. All Napoleon was doing was throwing away thousands more young French lives, inflicting bloody but not life-threatening wounds on the allied forces, and infuriating a certain Generalfeldmarschall Blücher, a fierce Prussian septuagenarian with a long memory and a bloodthirsty vengeful streak.

But if you are a Bonapartist historian, and your hero is about to lose his crown and be exiled for the first time, you need every victory you can get, even if no one else has ever heard of it.

VIII

In early 1814, Paris, the capital Napoleon was fighting desperately to defend, was also France's weakest point. His calls for new recruits fell on deaf ears there, or were drowned out by the babble of defeatist talk. While country peasants were rushing into battle armed only with scythes and pitchforks, hardly any Parisian men signed up to repel the invaders. On the contrary, keen to preserve their wealth and property, rich Parisians – and especially the old aristocracy, who had returned to France in droves when Napoleon

* Montereau, 80 kilometres south-east of Paris, is hoping to raise its profile by opening a Parc Napoléon in 2020. See the Epilogue, page 247, for more details.

offered them an amnesty – were doing their best to make peace with the allies. When he called on the city's population to man the barricades, the middle classes packed up their jewels and furniture and headed for the country.

While Napoleon was still in the east trying to harry his opponents into abandoning their advance, Paris signed a capitulation and handed the keys of the city to Czar Alexander, who entered the capital and went to stay with Talleyrand. His Russian troops were greeted with cheers.

Hearing of the surrender, Napoleon headed for his chateau at Fontainebleau, 70 kilometres south of Paris. But even here, he was surrounded by Parisians. They were his marshals and generals, who remembered the ruins of Moscow all too well and didn't want Paris to share the same fate. Marshal François-Joseph Lefebvre apparently told the Emperor, 'It's time to enjoy a rest. We own titles, houses, land – we don't want to get ourselves killed for you.' Hardly the kind of rousing speech Napoleon expected from his soldiers.

As if that weren't bad enough, Marshal Auguste Marmont, the man who was supposed to be mounting the defence of Paris, went over to the Austrians, giving up his 16,000 troops as prisoners. (They, incidentally, shouted 'Vive l'Empereur!' as they surrendered their weapons – though they surrendered them all the same.)

Napoleon's senior officers and former comrades-in-arms implored him to abdicate and end the fighting, and finally he gave in and wrote a letter of resignation, referring to himself, as he often did, in the third person: 'Since the allied powers have proclaimed that the Emperor Napoleon is the only obstacle to restoring peace in Europe, the Emperor Napoleon, true to his vow, declares that he renounces, for himself and his descendants, his right to the crowns of France and Italy, and that there is no personal sacrifice, even that of his life, that he is not ready to make in the interests of France.'

Napoleon did actually try to make the ultimate sacrifice, swallowing a poison that had been mixed for him during the Russian campaign. However, while he was saying farewell to his advisers, he vomited it all up, and his terrified doctor refused to give him anything stronger. The palace was full of pistols, muskets, bayonets and swords, but the gunpowder had been removed from Napoleon's personal pistols, and in any case he preferred poison, the favourite suicide method used in the tragic plays of France's greatest dramatist, Racine. When his stomach cramps began to subside, Napoleon decided that he was destined to live.

On 20 April, officers from the Russian, Austrian, Prussian and British armies arrived to attend the Emperor's official farewell. Napoleon walked out into the courtyard of the Château de Fontainebleau between two lines of his Old Guard in their tall bearskin hats and blue jackets, to make what was meant to be his final speech to his army:

'Soldiers of my Old Guard, I bid you adieu. For the past 20 years I have found you constantly on the paths of honour and glory . . . With men like you, our cause was not lost, but the war was interminable. There would have been civil war, which would only have brought France more misfortune. I therefore sacrifice all our interests to those of the homeland. I am leaving. You, my friends, must continue to serve France. Its happiness was always my only consideration.'

As his soldiers wept – even the British officer present was seen to loosen his stiff upper lip – Napoleon kissed a tricolour flag embroidered with the names of his victories and climbed into a carriage that immediately sped away.

In fact he was going to enjoy what Marshal Lefebvre had recently prescribed for him – a rest down on the Med, with the title of King of the island of Elba and a pension of two million francs a year, payable by the French government. Napoleon's wife and son had been more or less kidnapped by his Austrian father-in-law, Franz I, but he hoped that they would be able to meet up once he had proved to Europe that he was content to live as a simple retired soldier and, as he told his troops, 'write about the great things we did together'.

Early retirement on an island off the Tuscan coast at only forty-four, with a fat pension and plenty of time to write a book. What normal person wouldn't be content with that? The problem was that Napoleon wasn't a normal person.

Neither, one might say, are his fans, because they seem to regard even this humiliating exit – rejected by his own generals, with his wife and son snatched away by his in-laws – as a kind of victory. The grand *adieu* (the French consider it so important that it gets elevated to the plural, *adieux*) is re-enacted every year in Fontainebleau, which, like every other town with a connection to Napoleon, dubs itself a *ville impériale*. For the 200th anniversary in 2014 there was a week of commemoration culminating in a declamation of the sombre speech in the chateau courtyard. But most people, especially the Napoleon fans, found it difficult to be sombre, as is the case every year, for the simple reason that they know he came back . . .

IX

Elba ought to have been a very pleasant retirement home. The locals were delighted with their new resident, who had suddenly put their unknown island on the map. According to a certain Captain Jobit, on 4 May 1814, when Napoleon disembarked from the British frigate HMS *Undaunted*, he was met with cries of 'Vive l'Empereur!' and 'Vive Napoléon le Grand!' and given a banquet, fireworks and a display of the local ladies' *grande toilette* (which, as anyone who speaks French will know, is not a large lavatory but an outfit of smart clothing).

Napoleon's new subjects didn't mind that he had been unilaterally appointed their *souverain* (sovereign),* especially when he began to help them improve their economy. No doubt recalling his days at the military academy, he got the Elbans to plant Corsican chestnut trees on sloping land to prevent soil erosion, and to grow a variety of vegetables. He also encouraged the islanders to bottle and sell the

---

* Perhaps the landowners on Elba hadn't read the exact wording of Napoleon's exile agreement, which stipulated that he received 'for the rest of his life, the sovereignty and ownership' of the whole island.

naturally sparkling water from a spring. And, ever the organiser, he had the roads paved and set up a rubbish-collection system so that people would stop filling the streets with rotting refuse. The new sovereign even expanded Elba's borders by annexing a neighbouring unpopulated island and leaving a garrison of troops there. Not that Napoleon had begun to conscript the local men – rather unwisely, the allies had allowed him to take a thousand of his Guards along, so that it felt almost like being out on campaign again. Napoleon even slept on his old camp bed.

It would all have been fun except that he quickly realised his wife and son would never be joining him. In addition, he heard the sad news that his first wife Josephine had died, in tragically ironic circumstances. Apparently she had been giving Czar Alexander a guided tour of her rose garden – which was probably not a euphemism because she was a skilled creator of hybrid roses – when she contracted a chill that developed into pneumonia and what one French historian gruesomely describes as a 'gangrenous throat infection'.

Worse still for Napoleon was the news that France itself was also suffering from a gangrenous infection – its royal family, in the gout-ridden shape of King Louis XVIII, who had been imposed 'by foreign bayonets' and was now in the process of reducing the French army by 100,000 men, and retiring 12,000 officers on half pay.

Some of Napoleon's treacherous generals had been rewarded by Louis with new lands and titles, but they were all suffering the indignity of occupation. The hated Cossacks were camping on the Champs-Elysées, and the new British ambassador,

Wellington, the man who had kicked the French army out of Spain, was becoming famous for his anti-French jibes. At one dinner he was snubbed by a group of Frenchmen and, suspecting that there were ex-soldiers among them, quipped, "'Tis of no matter, I have seen their backs before.' Nothing hurts a French snob like a well-aimed insult. Especially an English insult.

The British and the other occupying forces were enjoying themselves too much. They paraded through Paris with Louis XVIII, their over-inflated puppet, whom even the Russian Czar secretly (or not so secretly) scorned – after a first state banquet with Louis in 1814, Alexander had announced that he had 'just met the most useless* man in Europe'. And much of this chaos was being fomented – organised, even – by the traitor Talleyrand, who, so Napoleon heard via his faithful informers, was now lobbying that the exiled Emperor of France be sent even further away – to the Azores.

By the end of 1814, Napoleon was already thinking that he had been away for long enough. France clearly needed him. He later told one of his marshals, 'I knew that the homeland was unhappy. I came back to free it from the émigrés and the Bourbons' (that is, the returning aristocrats and the exiled royal family).

Patriotism aside, it should also be pointed out that Napoleon was furious with Louis and Talleyrand because they had never paid him a cent of his huge pension. He

---

* Alexander used the French slang word *nul*, which means totally rubbish in all respects.

was having to finance his lavish lifestyle (he had a hundred servants on the island, as well as his Guards) out of his own money, which was now running low. Soon he would not have enough to pay his soldiers, and without them he would be defenceless against Talleyrand's attempts to kidnap him.

As any Frenchman knows, if you want to claim your pension rights, it is best to go straight to the central office in Paris. He had no choice but to leave Elba.

X

Like everything else in his life, Napoleon planned his escape with military precision. He ordered his grenadiers to start digging new flowerbeds, as if preparing for a long spring on the island. He had a ship, the *Inconstant* ('Unfaithful'), painted in British naval colours. Knowing that the island was infested with Talleyrand's spies disguised as monks, tourists and merchants, he started a rumour that he might be leaving for Naples. He even told his own men to put enough food and wine on the *Inconstant* for a trip to America.

On 26 February 1815, while the British military governor of the island, Colonel Neil Campbell, was away in Italy supposedly seeing a doctor but more probably visiting his mistress, Napoleon boarded the *Inconstant* and set sail for the French mainland with a flotilla of six smaller ships carrying his 1,000 soldiers. He told his men that he would 'retake [his] crown without spilling a single drop of blood'. He must have known that if it did come to a fight, his thousand-strong bodyguard wouldn't be much use against a million allied invaders.

He had already written the speech he intended to give to the nation:

'People of France, a prince imposed by a temporarily victorious enemy is relying upon a few enemies of the people who have been condemned by all French governments for the last 25 years. During my exile, I have heard your complaints and your wishes. You have been demanding the government of your choice. I have crossed the sea and am here to reclaim my rights, which are also yours.'

And he didn't only mean his pension.

Napoleon's triumphant march north to Paris is the favourite story among pro-Bonaparte historians. They savour every detail. Reading their accounts, you get to know everything Napoleon ate en route (half a roast chicken in the village of Roccavignon near Grasse, for example, and roast duck and olives in Sisteron, in the foothills of the Alps), how little he slept (he would set off every morning at four a.m.), and the flattering speeches he gave in every town he crossed ('my dearest wish was to arrive with the speed of an eagle in this good town of Gap/Grenoble/what's its name again?').

The descriptions of how French soldiers, supposedly in the service of Louis XVIII, defied their officers and joined Napoleon are the stuff of a propaganda film. These are the Bonapartists' fondest memories.

Just outside Grenoble, for example, the returning Emperor was faced by 700 soldiers sent to stop his advance. Obeying orders, they raised their muskets and pointed them at Napoleon. Telling his musicians to play 'La Marseillaise', the revolutionary song that had been the exit music for Louis XVIII's predecessor in 1789, Napoleon walked alone towards the line of 700 rifles. When he was within easy shooting range, he opened his famous grey overcoat and called out, 'If there is among you one soldier who wants to kill his Emperor, here I am.'

In reply came a volley of 'Vive l'Empereur!' The order to fire was ignored and the men rushed to greet Napoleon. Boney was back.

In Lyon, there was a similar scene of defiance. Louis XVIII's brother Charles came to lead the defence of the city. He inspected the 1,500-strong garrison, who were treated to a patriotic speech by their commanding officer and then ordered to shout 'Vive le Roi!' None obeyed. Charles went out into the ranks and politely asked a dragoon to give the shout. The man bravely stayed mute, and the King's brother leapt straight into his carriage and left for Paris. The monarchy, he realised, was finished (again).

Back in Paris, Napoleon's old friend Marshal Ney was less supportive than the lower ranks. He declared that the fallen Emperor 'deserved to be brought back [to Paris] in an iron cage'.* He told Louis that 'every Frenchman should repel him', and suggested to the King that his troops would be more loyal if Louis himself was seen going into battle.

* This is a famous quotation that ensures Ney a decidedly chilly reception whenever Bonapartist historians are describing his actions at Waterloo, as we shall see in Chapter 3.

Not on a horse, of course (it would have needed an elephant to carry him), but perhaps carried on a litter? No doubt aware that his bulk would make a large target for Napoleon's guns, Louis decided that it was wiser for him to escape back into exile.

This all sounds like a hero's return for Napoleon, but it would be a mistake to ignore the voices of dissent, even among his supporters. One officer, a certain Colonel Le Bédoyère, a veteran of the Russian campaign, brought his soldiers over to Napoleon but warned him, 'No more ambition, Sire, no more despotism. Your Majesty must abandon the system of conquests and extreme power that brought misfortune to France and yourself.'

The newspapers of the time were also largely against Napoleon. Louis XVIII had only recently granted freedom of the press, and the editors didn't want to lose it again to their deposed dictator. The papers embarked on a campaign of disinformation, claiming for example that Napoleon had been stopped at Digne in the French Alps and chased off by local peasants. The problem was that by the time a report was published in the papers, rumours had outrun it. On the day Napoleon was supposedly turned back at Digne, he was already 200 kilometres north of there, in Grenoble.

What is not always pointed out in French history books is that Napoleon chose a Hannibal-like route through the French Alps because he was afraid of meeting hostile crowds in large towns along the south coast, like Toulon, where he had suppressed the pro-royalist revolt in 1793.

In a recent study of private letters written at the time, a

French historian called Aurélien Lignereux revealed that Napoleon was right to be afraid of opposition. Ordinary middle-class French people were reacting to the news of his return with trepidation. They saw it as yet another upheaval, and suspected that war would be around the corner yet again.

But for the moment at least, Napoleon didn't need to bother about the opinion of the common *bourgeois* – he knew that they weren't going to put together an army of umbrella-waving ladies and pen-wielding solicitors to oppose his return. And he knew this because he had stopped a carriage carrying mail from Paris, and had the letters read by his aides. Even 200 years ago, the war of information was a vital part of a politician's life.

XI

When Napoleon arrived in Paris on 20 March 1815, school-children greeted the news by cheering and beating out a celebration drumroll on their desktops. Perhaps they knew that they were safe from conscription, though it probably wasn't a good idea to be too proficient at drumming – Napoleon's armies sent young drummer boys into the front lines, to be shot at just like the adults.

The politicians weren't quite as welcoming as the school-children, and Napoleon discovered that the perfidious English had made their mark during the brief occupation of Paris. France's parliament was now dominated by English-style liberals who told Napoleon that the population would back him only if he agreed to a new constitution. They demanded that he maintain the British-style two-house parliamentary system set up by Louis XVIII, with a Chambre des Pairs (a house of hereditary peers) and a Chambre des Députés (consisting of MPs elected for five years). He also had to confirm the freedom of the press, and accept criticism of his regime. The old-style emperor-god was a thing of the past.

Unwillingly, Napoleon accepted the concessions demanded of him, though he refused to call this a new constitution, and dubbed the changes the Acte Additionnel, as though it were merely an afterthought to his former regime.

He also had to shrug off the humiliation of disastrous elections, which saw huge abstention rates (especially among the silent *bourgeois* majority), and a wave of liberal, anti-Bonapartist MPs and mayors elected or re-elected (80 per cent of the local officials put in place by Louis XVIII's regime were confirmed in office). Napoleon might have started to wonder why he hadn't remained on Elba as the island's uncontested sovereign. As it was, he contented himself with dismissing parliamentary debates as 'vain chatter'.

There was one consolation, though – he did get his way with his re-investiture. On 1 June, on the Champ de Mars in front of his old Ecole Militaire, Napoleon held a stupendously self-congratulatory ceremony before 400,000 spectators, including 50,000 soldiers. For the occasion he designed himself a new imperial costume – a red tunic, a cape lined with ermine, white trousers and stockings, and a Roman emperor's crown. His soldiers, though, weren't happy: they wanted to be reunited with their beloved general, not a dandy in fancy dress.

Not that Napoleon was over-keen to get back into military uniform. He knew that the most he could hope for now was to reign unopposed over France. Rekindling the war against the allies would be suicidal. He made a speech admitting as much: 'I have given up my idea of a great Empire that I had only just begun to build. My aim was to organise a federal European system that matched the spirit of the century and favoured the advancement of our civilisation.* My goal now is simply to increase France's prosperity by strengthening public freedom.' Sadly for Napoleon, his old nemesis Talleyrand was not willing to let this happen. Ever the tireless anti-Bonaparte campaigner, when news came through that Napoleon had landed in France, Talleyrand was in Vienna meeting with Metternich, Czar Alexander and Wellington. He immediately began to whip up outrage among the allies, declaring that Napoleon was 'the disturber of world peace'. In no time at all, Russia, Prussia, Austria and Britain had promised to launch their armies against Napoleon, guaranteeing at least 150,000 soldiers each.

Napoleon sent a peace envoy to Metternich, and a placatory letter to England's Prince Regent, but both were ignored. On 7 June he made a speech in Paris, informing

---

* A federal European system geared to the advancement of French civilisation – 200 years later, via the EU, France is still trying to make Napoleon's wish come true.

his people that 'It is possible that the first duty of a prince will soon call me to lead the children of the nation in a fight for our homeland. The army and I will do our duty.'

Dominique de Villepin, France's Prime Minister from 2005 to 2007, supports Napoleon in this resolve to fight. 'Governing,' he writes in his book *Les Cent Jours* (referring to Napoleon's 100-day return to power in 1815),* 'does not mean endlessly negotiating in the hope of finding a compromise. It means deciding. Governing implies cool-headedness, initiative and responsibility.' It is the usual Bonapartist refrain: Napoleon, they say, desired only peace, but when he recognised the inevitability of war, like the hero he was, he could not shy away from it.

The facts are more banal. Surrounded by enemies both at home and abroad, Napoleon had no choice but to accept the impossible odds if he wanted to hang on to power. The long journey from his first victory against the British fleet in Toulon in 1793 had come to its climax. Almost twenty years of glory, followed by two and a half in which he had lost two whole armies and his throne. He had known total power, self-inflicted disaster, exile, a glorious return, and now he had to fight one last great battle to decide his ultimate fate.

---

* Incidentally, Villepin was so inspired by Napoleon in his own political career that when he was appointed Prime Minister, he gave himself 'a hundred days to restore confidence' in President Jacques Chirac's right-wing regime. Sadly, Villepin's first measure, a law that gave employers the right to fire workers under the age of twenty-five, provoked a national strike and rioting, and dashed his hopes of running for the presidency.

Napoleon, and Europe itself, was ready for Waterloo.

The improbable thing is that Napoleon thought he could win – although even that is less improbable than the way his admirers still allege that he actually did.

2

AT WATERLOO, NAPOLEON ALSO HAD TO FIGHT GOD AND HIS OWN GENERALS

'Napoléon est le héros parfait . . . Il n'eut pas une pensée qui ne fît une action, et toutes ses actions furent grandes . . .'

'Napoleon is the perfect hero . . . He never had a thought that he did not put into action, and all his actions were great . . .'

– nineteenth-century French writer Anatole France

I

Waterloo is probably the most-analysed battle in history. Every musket shot and cannonball of 18 June 1815 has been debated, ballistically tested, computer-generated and re-enacted – especially by Bonapartists trying to extract positive conclusions from the debacle.

Countless veterans of the actual battle emerged from the mud and gore to tell their stories, which are often self-aggrandising and almost always partly inaccurate, because each one is of necessity just a personal snapshot of the events of the day. Over the past two centuries, these have been slotted together like the odd-shaped pieces of a thousand different jigsaw puzzles.

The accounts of what went on at Waterloo include those of Wellington and Napoleon, both of whom wrote their official reports while the wounded were still trying to crawl off the battlefield. Predictably, both men's reports are biased – Wellington's by old-fashioned English understatement and Napoleon's by the need to stress that he did not have to give up his emperor's cloak just yet, because his army could regroup and carry on the fight.

In most British versions of the battle, there is an understandable undercurrent of triumphalism. Meanwhile many French accounts, including those by veterans, tend towards a more puzzling conclusion. Someone lost the battle, they seem to admit, but one thing's for sure: it wasn't Napoleon.

His defenders explain away the disaster by blaming it on everyone and everything except *l'Empereur* himself. They point an accusing pen at God, the weather, destiny, history, traitors, deserters, the generals, the contours of the battlefield, the type of mud, the dense smoke, the food, piles, a urinary problem, syphilis, and – of course – British cheating.

So who or what exactly was to blame for it all going so wrong for Napoleon?

II

Among Napoleon's many sayings on the subject of fighting was: 'In war, as in love, to get the job done, you have to get up close.' But tender-hearted he was not. For him, war was all about merciless, focused attack.

He had reinvented warfare using what Dominique de Villepin calls his three weapons – cannon, bayonets and horses. He would launch a diversionary assault on his opponent's left or right flank while his artillery would batter what he considered the weakest point of the opposing lines, and skirmishers would snipe at key officers and gunners. Then, depending on the terrain, the cavalry or infantry would charge, the opposing lines would break into a rout, and finally the cavalry would mop up with their sabres and lances, playing dandelion cutters with the fleeing soldiers to ensure that no one would be around to fight the following day.

This was the theory, and it often worked in practice, which was why the Russians had been so careful to avoid face-to-face confrontation in 1812.

Napoleon's charges were as terrifying as his artillery onslaughts. The heavy cavalry would trot forward slowly, an impenetrable mass of snorting horses and growling Frenchmen. The infantry would begin its advance with linked arms and march straight into musket or cannon fire, each fallen man instantly replaced by another. Then, nearing the lines, they would point their bayonets straight at the enemy's hearts and close in for the kill. The idea was to give the opposing army plenty of time to panic in the face of the wave of doom bearing down on them, and run.

Napoleon's footsoldiers called these charges a *déjeuner à la fourchette* – a 'fork lunch' – and one of his army's many slogans was 'the Old Guard only fights with the bayonet'. French historians describe Napoleon's battles with all the glee of *Dad's Army*'s Corporal Jones' catchphrase 'They don't like it up 'em'. It's no coincidence that the most common words in French Napoleonic histories are *Empereur*, *gloire* (glory), *patrie* (homeland) and *baïonette*. Bonapartist historians delight in the butchery inflicted on France's enemies by Napoleon's fearless troops.

Before Waterloo, Napoleon was looking forward to an attack along these lines. He told his general Maximilien Foy, 'The battle that is about to come will save France and be famous in the annals of history. I will bring my artillery into play, I will send my cavalry into the charge to force the enemy to show themselves, and when I know exactly where the British troops are, I will march straight at them with my Old Guard.'

In the end, the only bit he got wrong was the prediction that he would save France. (Although some French people would of course dispute even that.)

Napoleon knew that several armies, in total about a million men, were converging on him at once: the Spanish and Portuguese from the south-west, the Austrians and Italians from the south-east, and the Anglo–Dutch/Prussian/Russian coalition from the north. His only hope was to go out and face them. Marching into attack kept the morale of his soldiers high, and he knew that the French people would not back a leader who allowed raping, pillaging troops to return to French soil. No matter that his Army of the North was only 128,000-strong, half of them new recruits, and that in the first part of his defence campaign he would be going up against more than 200,000 allied troops. He ordered his army to march into Belgium, and at four a.m. on 12 June, he got into his carriage (ironically called a *berline* in French, after the capital of Prussia) and went to join them.

Napoleon dictated a proclamation to be read to his men on 15 June, reminding them that it was the anniversary of his victories over the Austrians at Marengo (1800) and the Russians at Friedland (1807), which, he said, 'twice decided the fate of Europe'. However, he went on, 'we were too generous. We believed the promises and vows of the princes that we left on their thrones. Today, allied against us, they are threatening France's most sacred rights and independence . . . One moment of prosperity* has blinded them . . . If they enter into France it will be to find a grave there!'

III

Napoleon's strategy was to use speed, thrusting his troops between Wellington and Blücher's armies, hoping to push them apart and destroy first one then the other. According to French historian Jean-Claude Damamme, Napoleon was

---

* Probably a reference to the bad British habit of selling Europe cheap cotton, cutlery, tea, coffee and sugar. Napoleon presumably hoped that his soldiers were opposed to the idea of low-cost beverages.

banking on even more than the effect of surprise. He thought that the alliance was one-sided and that Wellington was, Damamme alleges, 'cautious and selfish, like any Englishman, and [would] show no haste in coming to his ally's aid'. A big enough rift would end the war in the north in Napoleon's favour.

At first, his plan seemed to be working. On 16 June, his army fought two simultaneous battles, at Ligny and Quatre-Bras, two villages a few kilometres south of Waterloo.

Napoleon began by sending Marshal Ney – who had been welcomed back into the fold despite his remarks about the need to lock Napoleon in a metal cage – to take a vital crossroads at Quatre-Bras, which was held by some of Wellington's Dutch troops. Surprisingly, although it was only lightly occupied, Ney dithered, and didn't attack until after lunch, when Wellington had had time to send reinforcements. Fighting went on until dark, by which time nothing had been achieved on either side except around 4,000 casualties each.

Meanwhile in and around the village of Ligny a few kilometres to the east, Napoleon began hammering Blücher, and used a sweeping attack by his Old Guard to break the Prussian lines. The battle was a bloodbath, with the French losing about 7,000 dead or wounded and the Prussians 20,000 – all in one afternoon of crashing cannon fire and vicious street fighting to gain control of the village (which was still occupied by innocent Belgian civilians). Blücher himself almost died in the battle when his horse was shot from under him and he was ridden over by the French cavalry. Amazingly for a seventy-two-year-old, he not only survived, but vowed to fight the next battle.

The problem for Napoleon was that despite a clear victory at Ligny and an honourable draw at Quatre-Bras, he had not managed to smash either Wellington's or Blücher's armies. He could have inflicted far more damage on the Prussians if he had pursued them, and might have beaten Wellington soundly if Ney had been quicker off the mark. But the worst thing was that, contrary to his expectations, the Prussians did not retreat east along their supply lines. They went north, sticking close to Wellington. The Iron Duke, meanwhile, withdrew and regrouped at a place he knew well – Waterloo.

This is where Bonapartists, desperate to defend Napoleon's record as one of history's winners, allege that the perfidious Brits showed their true character: despite all their nonsense about fair play and giving everyone a sporting chance, the English cheated. The implication is that if a victory is won unfairly, surely it doesn't really count as a victory. The Bonapartist argument here is that not only had the British government been financing Napoleon's enemies for years, skewing the odds against him; now Wellington had a whole day to position his men on ground that he had reconnoitred *a full year earlier*.

During the campaign to oust Napoleon in 1814, Wellington had shrewdly scouted out likely sites for a face-off with the aggressive *Empereur*, and recognised the strategic importance of this crossroads just south of Brussels. He knew that the ridge running across the main road to the Belgian capital – a plateau known as the Mont Saint-Jean – would provide cover for his men when Napoleon began firing his cannons. It would also enable him to conceal the true strength of his army from prying French telescopes. Furthermore, even though the surrounding fields were not as sloping or (yet) as muddy as those at Agincourt and Crécy, the British army would, almost exactly 400 years after Agincourt, be standing on a ridge waiting for Frenchmen to trudge towards them. It was a good omen.

Some people might see this foresight on Wellington's part as great military tactics, but most French historians agree that grabbing the high ground gave him an unfair advantage. Wellington had not so much moved the goalposts as decided where they would be set up in the first place. It was not fair play at all (even though the concept of fair play is so alien to the French that they don't have a word for it – they call it *le fair-play*).

As a result of this British 'cheating', the French would be advancing uphill across what Victor Hugo, one of Napoleon's most outspoken defenders, famously called a 'morne plaine' – a bleak, sad, dismal plain, almost the equivalent of Macbeth's 'blasted heath'. And the fields south of Waterloo were about to get blasted in no small measure.

IV

Nature, then, favoured the English at Waterloo, just as the early November frost had enabled the Russians to evict the French from Moscow. But this was hardly surprising, because in many French eyes, God was against Napoleon.* He had been helping the Brits before the battle even started. In a book called *Histoire des derniers jours de la Grande Armée*, a Waterloo veteran called Hippolyte de Mauduit wrote that General Vandamme was late arriving at Ligny, but would have been there five hours earlier 'had fate not wanted the officer bringing the order to break his leg en route'. Without 'this fateful accident', Mauduit concludes, Napoleon's 'skilful plans' would have resulted in outright victory against Wellington and Blücher. But 'God decided otherwise'. And Mauduit was at Waterloo with the Old Guard, so he should know.

Dominique de Villepin entitles the section in his book on the events of 18 June 'Waterloo ou la crucifixion', again giving a religious tinge to what was purely a battle for political supremacy in Europe. Perhaps he feels that God sacrificed Napoleon to atone for our sins, or even that God was annoyed with Napoleon for attacking on a Sunday? After all, one of the charges laid against Joan of Arc by the religious court that eventually sentenced her to death for wearing men's clothes was that she had fought battles on the Sabbath. Why should Napoleon be excused?

But it is Victor Hugo who argues most strongly that Napoleon's fate was decided somewhere beyond the clouds. In the vivid description of Waterloo in his novel *Les*

---

* Since the Revolution, France has officially been an atheist country, but the French still look to God whenever they need someone to blame for something that has no obvious cause. That is, when they can't blame the English, the Germans, the Americans or other French people.

Misérables, Hugo declares bluntly that 'his [Napoleon's] fall was decided. He bothered God.'

The problem seems to boil down to a rivalry between two alpha males – God and Napoleon. 'Was it possible for Napoleon to win this battle?' Hugo asks, using French writers' favourite stylistic tic, the rhetorical question. 'We answer: no,' he goes on, modestly referring to himself in the plural. 'Why? Because of Wellington? Because of Blücher? No. Because of God.'

The trouble with Napoleon was that he was just too great, Hugo explains. 'It was time for this vast man to fall . . . the excessive importance of this man in human destiny was unbalancing things . . . Waterloo wasn't a battle. It was a change in direction of the universe.' What Hugo seems to be suggesting is that God was getting a bit jealous of Napoleon, and decided to dampen his squib. As we know, Napoleon's favourite weapon was the cannon. So all God had to do was put them out of action . . .

It rains a lot in south-western Belgium. It rains every month in an average year, with peaks in July and August. June is the fourth rainiest month of the year. Even so, there are French commentators who see the downpour that began at about 2.30 p.m. on 17 June 1815 and lasted all through the night as some kind of freakish divine intervention. Hugo says that 'if it hadn't rained on the night of 17-18 June, the future of Europe would have been different. A few raindrops more or less felled Napoleon.'

Dominique de Villepin backs this up, saying that 'when

men didn't compromise his [Napoleon's] battle plans, the elements did'. Villepin, like other Bonapartist historians, quotes *Grande Armée* veterans complaining about the atrocious weather. One of these is the chief of staff to General Maximilien Foy, an officer called Marie Jean Baptiste Lemonnier-Delafosse (though for obvious reasons the 'Marie' is usually omitted when discussing his military career). Captain Lemonnier-Delafosse, like so many Waterloo veterans, wrote his memoirs, in which he was scathing about the conditions of Belgium's roads in the wet.

After beating the Prussians at Ligny, Lemonnier-Delafosse notes, Napoleon wanted to regroup his armies and send all his men against Wellington, who was retreating towards Waterloo. But 'the road was a veritable river . . . already full of potholes thanks to the English army that we were following. Infantry, cavalry, artillery, etc., all on the same road, leaving those at the back in the most terrible mud.' As other armies have found out since, Flanders can play havoc with military footwear.

Lemonnier-Delafosse goes on to complain about the drenching he got in the hours that followed: 'The night of the 17th to the 18th June seemed to foreshadow the misfortunes of the day. An uninterrupted violent downpour meant that the army could not enjoy a single minute of rest. To make things even worse, the bad roads hindered the delivery of supplies, and most of the men – both common soldiers and officers – were deprived of food.'

As we all know, the Almighty can inflict no worse hardship on humankind than to deprive a Frenchman of his dinner, but Lemonnier-Delafosse seems to have had faith in a higher power – Napoleon: 'As dawn broke, catching sight of the Emperor, [the men] called out to him, announcing that they were ready to rise to another victory.' The trouble was, though, that the heaven-sent deluge had clearly put victory out of even Napoleon's reach. The mud made all manoeuvres impossible, and Lemonnier-Delafosse concludes that 'If the Emperor had been able to start the battle at five in the morning, by mid-day Lord Wellington would have been beaten.'*

Sergeant Hippolyte de Mauduit told a similar story: 'While marching backwards and forwards during that terrible night, everything was confusion . . . We searched in vain for our generals and our officers in the darkness and pounding rain. We had to climb through hedges and across ravines . . . Our overcoats and trousers were dragging two or three pounds of mud; many men had lost their boots and arrived at the bivouac with bare feet.'

Thousands of French soldiers were forced to sleep out in the open. Lieutenant Jacques-François Martin painted a surprisingly humorous picture of what must have been a hellish night for him: 'It was as black as the inside of an oven, the rain was falling in torrents, and, to make us even happier, the regiment was posted in a ploughed field that had become totally flooded. And it was here that we were supposed to get some sweet repose. No wood, no straw, no

---

* Note that for good measure, Lemonnier-Delafosse demotes Wellington from a Duke to a Lord.

food, and no way of getting any. But at least we couldn't complain about the bed. No one could say it was hard. As soon as we lay down, we sank softly into the mud . . . It was a little chilly, but we had the satisfaction of knowing that every time we turned over, the rain would wash the side of our uniform that had been lying in the mud.'

Captain Pierre-Charles Duthilt, a battalion leader, was on the right flank of Napoleon's army, near a coal mine, and had similar problems. He remembered that the road was 'covered by black mud that had been diluted and turned into ink. It made our cavalry unrecognisable. The uniforms, the men and the horses were stained from head to foot, just a mass of mud.'

Duthilt also complained about the food: 'The bread, rice and brandy destined for the soldiers had been stolen or spoilt . . . Cooking had been done quickly, in villages far away from the road, and the supply was insufficient . . . The English army, on the other hand, had everything it needed, especially liquids of all sorts.'

The French historian Jean-Claude Damamme agrees with Duthilt that the common British soldiers were living the good life out in the rain-soaked country. They had plundered the villages and farms for improvised building materials, he says, and were sheltering under carts, doors, shutters and tables.

It seems hard to believe that God would provide exclusively for the *Anglais*, or that Napoleon's army was so respectful of Belgian farmers' property that they didn't try to pilfer anything that would keep the rain off. An anonymous French account of the battle confirms this. *Relation fidèle et détaillée de la dernière campagne de Buonaparte, terminée par la bataille de Mont-Saint-Jean, dite de Waterloo ou de la Belle-Alliance, par un témoin oculaire* ('a faithful and detailed account of Bonaparte's last campaign, ending in the Battle of Mont Saint-Jean, known as Waterloo or Belle Alliance, by an eye witness') was probably written by a disaffected officer, to judge by his use of the Corsican-Italian form of Napoleon's name, Buonaparte, which he had changed to Bonaparte when he rose to prominence on the French mainland. The writer alleges that that night, French soldiers 'plundered houses and, under cover of searching for food, smashed doors, broke into cupboards, mistreated the peasants and grabbed anything they wanted. We were campaigning, and the war couldn't be fought without us, they reasoned, so they could do whatever they wanted.'

Of course, even among the French, conditions got better the higher you rose in the ranks, as General Victor-Albert Dessales found out to his cost: 'It rained abundantly during the night, and I had to give up my billet to the comte d'Erlon [his superior officer]. I therefore spent the night in a bivouac. By morning I was soaking wet, and if I hadn't found a carriage in the park, I wouldn't have been able to change, which would have been most disagreeable.'

Napoleon himself spent the night in a charming farm-house a few kilometres south of the next day's battlefield. Today, Le Caillou ('The Pebble') is a museum containing, among other artefacts, one of the *Empereur*'s camp beds, and the actual table where he breakfasted on 18 June with his chiefs of staff.

Maintaining the religious theme of the whole campaign, a plaque on the farmhouse wall states (in French) that 'Le Caillou was saved and converted into a place of pilgrimage by the historian Lucien Laudy'.* And Napoleon himself attracts large numbers of pilgrims to the farm where, on the night of 17 June, he took shelter in a tiny room – Damamme specifies that his bedroom on the ground floor measured only 6.20 metres by 4.65, though he fails to mention the rather grand fireplace that must have kept the place cosy on that stormy night. There, Damamme says, Napoleon lay on his camp bed and ate a meal off the farmer's humble plates – his crockery wagon had not made it through the mud. The farmer's plates have been preserved in the museum, and aren't all that humble at all. They are white and very sturdy, less refined than Napoleon's usual monogrammed porcelain or silver plate but as good as anything outside a chateau of the times.

Despite his lack of sleep – this was Saturday and Napoleon had been on the road, travelling or fighting, since three a.m. on Monday – the novelist/historian Max Gallo claims that the Emperor could not lie down. He depicts Napoleon pacing around the house, suffering under the weight of responsibility, gazing fondly on the French officers bedded down in the rest of the house and the barn. Being a man of the people, he also goes to the door and looks out at his soldiers tramping

* Laudy was a local historian and passionate defender of the Waterloo battle site against desecration by farmers and developers. He lived in Le Caillou farmhouse until his death in 1948, after which the farm was bought by La Société Belge des Etudes Napoléoniennes.

past in the rain, 'their uniforms soaked, their weapons wet, their bodies slumped in exhaustion'. And according to most French histories of the battle, Napoleon himself was not exactly feeling full of *haricots* himself.

V

It wasn't just sleep deprivation that was causing Napoleon's physical problems, we are told. During the night, Gallo has him trembling and 'breathing badly, as though his chest were being crushed'. Most Bonapartist historians who try to explain away the events of the next day point to some sickness or other that was diminishing Napoleon's normally superhuman stocks of energy and inventiveness.

The most popular theory is that Napoleon suffered from piles. This sounds like a rumour invented to amuse the toilet-obsessed Brits, but French commentators seem to confirm the stories. In *Les Misérables*, Victor Hugo coyly refers to the Emperor's haemorrhoids as 'local pains', and in his book *Histoire de la Campagne de 1815 – Waterloo*, the nineteenth-century military historian Jean-Baptiste-Adolphe Charras describes them as 'atrocious pains on the day of Waterloo'. Napoleon's brother Jérôme, who fought at Waterloo, mentions the piles explicitly in his memoirs, and the Emperor's surgeon, Barron Larrey, is known to have treated the imperial backside with hot wet cloths just after the Battle of Ligny. It seems certain that on the 18th, the Emperor was at the very least feeling some posterior tenderness.

Strange, then, to read so many accounts of Napoleon

riding around the battlefield for much of the day, going out on his horse to get a closer look at troop movements, even galloping when it was necessary. This would have been agony for a man with acute haemorrhoids, especially because there is never any mention of a customised soft saddle.

The conclusions are obvious: either Napoleon was not suffering from serious piles and therefore had one less excuse for losing the battle, or – the version offered up by Bonapartist historians – he heroically ignored the agony and soldiered on.

Max Gallo's biographical novel is full of scenes in which Napoleon has to think of the nation and overcome his personal pain. Gallo also makes the clearest, and most gruesome, reference to piles. He imagines Napoleon in his carriage on the way to Belgium, in agony: 'A sharp pain ripped through his stomach. Then it felt as though thick black blood, heavy and burning-hot, were flowing through his lower body, swelling the veins until they were fit to burst. He had the humiliating, exhausting obsession that, instead of urine and shit, he was going to start spouting blood.' Ouch indeed.

And piles are by no means the only physical affliction blamed for hampering Napoleon's performance at Waterloo. Some say he was suffering from acromegaly, an imbalance of the pituitary gland which can cause lethargic over-confidence (much like the condition that seems to inflict England footballers during any major international tournament). Others have diagnosed a 'dysuric problem' – in other words, trouble urinating. Jean-Baptiste-Adolphe Charras goes further, suggesting that the *Empereur* might have been suffering from syphilis, or as Charras euphemistically puts it, 'an accidental disease that gave Napoleon great discomfort . . . Napoleon had contracted the sickness that killed King François I'.*

Whatever the actual source of Napoleon's aches and pains on 18 June 1815, he seems to have forgotten about them during the fighting. The sound and smell of cannon fire, and the prospect of a violent death or – even worse – humiliation and dishonour seem to have enlivened him. At the height of the battle, sitting calmly on his horse, with cannonballs and grapeshot falling all around him, he famously told one of his young aides-de-camp, who was ducking his head and moving around, 'Stay still, my friend, a gunshot will kill you just as easily from behind as from in front – and cause a much uglier wound.'

The real problem for Napoleon, according to his admirers, was that the other commanders of his army were by no means as sharply focused on the job in hand.

VI

As a rain-free dawn broke on the morning of the Battle of Waterloo, most ordinary French soldiers seem to have been looking forward to a fight. At least a few explosions might warm things up a bit. Many of them were annoyed to discover that their cartridges were wet – they were carrying large

---

* Generations of French history teachers have taught that François died of syphilis, but more recently it has been suggested that he was suffering from horrendously painful abscesses caused by urogenital tuberculosis.

stocks of ammunition in their backpacks because Napoleon had rightly feared that the supply wagons would not keep up. Now, though, the men were apparently afraid that they would run out of dry powder during the fighting. However, the situation must have been very similar over on the other side of the front line, and this 'damp cartridge' problem is reminiscent of the frequently repeated French claim about Agincourt – that their crossbowmen couldn't reply to the English archers because their crossbow strings were wet.

Meanwhile, the rain-sodden, mud-encrusted young Lieutenant Jacques-François Martin and his men were apparently in astonishing good humour. Martin wrote jokingly that 'Next morning, bright and early, we jumped out of bed' – he had slept in the mud, remember – 'and after preening ourselves, the well-rested soldiers went off in search of everything we needed. Soon we were able to light a fire and grill some beef cutlets that were delicious. And we drank plenty – water was not exactly lacking. Thus refreshed, our weapons cleaned, we waited impatiently for the order to move.'

Of course the order didn't come, thanks to the mud. Napoleon – who by all accounts had managed to grab some sleep in his camp bed – had decided that the Prussians would not arrive on the battlefield until 4.30 p.m. He had time to beat the English first. At dawn, around 4.30 a.m., he gave orders for his army to be ready to attack at nine. As he recalled in his memoirs, 'I saw the weak rays of the sun which, before it went down again, would highlight the defeat of the English army.' Sadly though, the sun had not yet dried out the fields and his cannons couldn't be moved.

Neither, throughout the day to come, could several of his commanders. Their inactivity and lack of decisiveness, or sudden bursts of badly directed energy, are usually given by Bonapartist historians – including Napoleon himself – as the main reason for losing at Waterloo.

At the re-enactment of the Battle of Brienne le Château in May 2014, I witnessed a scene that illustrates French feeling on this delicate matter. At one of the many bookstalls devoted to French literature on Napoleon and his campaigns, a man was selling a glossy new picture book that contained reproductions of all the paintings depicting the *Empereur*'s famous battles. It was a very tall, very thick book. Two old ladies were leafing through, and suddenly stopped.

'Oh, le voilà!' one of them exclaimed – there he is.

The bookseller sidled over to ask whom they had spotted. The women closed the book and one of them explained, just loud enough for an attentive eavesdropper to overhear, that they were sisters, and were descended from one of Napoleon's marshals, 'but we don't like to say his name out loud because he's not very popular'. The bookseller leaned in close and encouraged them to confide, to no avail. But it occurred to me that it didn't really matter – almost none of the French commanders came out of Waterloo covered in glory.

The problems at the top had started even before the battle. At dawn on 15 June, General Louis-Auguste Bourmont deserted to the enemy with his general staff. He wrote a letter to Napoleon explaining that he did not 'want to play a part in establishing bloody despotism in France'. The only consolation for Bonapartists is that Blücher refused to talk to Bourmont, even though he had donned the white royalist cockade to avoid getting shot at as he approached enemy lines. Blücher is said to have explained his snub in delightful soldierly language: 'Hundsfott bleibt Hundsfott!' – literally 'once a dog's vagina, always a dog's vagina'.

Napoleon would probably have agreed, though perhaps he ought to have had his doubts about Bourmont's loyalty much earlier. The man was a royalist who had fought against the Revolution and served as an envoy to the King-in-exile Louis XVIII. Bourmont had also been imprisoned for plotting against Napoleon at the start of his reign. He had then been reinstated as a soldier and served in Italy, but without a command of his own. Napoleon had even written a letter to the Minister of War asking 'what would our troops think about being commanded by such a man?' Despite all this, Napoleon made Bourmont a general, and here he was defecting instead of leading his troops into battle.

Napoleon ought to have had similar doubts about Ney, but the man who wanted to put the Emperor in a cage was recalled to duty just a few days before Waterloo. This had immediate consequences, as Ney's new aide-de-camp Colonel Heymès remembered: 'The troops were exhausted after a 20-hour march. The marshal [Ney] didn't know the names of his generals or colonels. He didn't even know how many men were in each regiment.'

Michel Ney was a grand figure in 1815, a tall, forty-six-year-old red-headed cavalry officer who had risen through the ranks because of his fearlessness, and earned the affectionate nickname 'tomato head'. He had distinguished himself in Austria, Prussia and Russia, and survived being hit in the neck by a Russian bullet. But he was hot-tempered, and had fallen out so badly with his fellow marshals during the Spanish campaign that Napoleon had brought him back to Paris to train troops.

Ney was the first marshal to defect to the royalists in 1814, but had returned to Napoleon's camp even before Louis XVIII fled France in March 1815. There was no doubting his courage or his patriotism, but by June 1815 he was a battle-weary and politically confused man who had apparently warned Napoleon face to face not to 'play the tyrant'. Not exactly a reliable brother-in-arms.

One of the men Ney had fallen out with in Spain was Marshal Jean-de-Dieu Soult. The two were the same age, but never got on. Soult had fought under Napoleon to win the great victory at Austerlitz in 1805 but, like Ney, quickly turned royalist in 1814. He then called Napoleon a 'usurper and opportunist' and became Louis XVIII's Minister of War, during which time he actually implemented a policy to reduce numbers in the army. Not a natural Bonapartist, it would seem. Even so, Napoleon appointed him chief of staff of his army, one of his closest advisers and aides-de-camp.

Meanwhile, in preparation for Waterloo, Napoleon entrusted the job of keeping the Prussians at bay in the east to Emmanuel de Grouchy, a marshal about whom almost all French historians are scathing. One of his subordinates, a certain Colonel Chapuis, is often quoted as saying: 'It was clear that providence had condemned us, and chosen Marshal Grouchy to punish us.'

The story about Grouchy that has gone down in French legend is the tale of his carefree strawberry breakfast on 18 June: while he should have been scouring the countryside in an attempt to pinpoint Blücher's exact position, he broke camp at eight a.m. (several hours after the usual wake-up call of Napoleonic commanders) and enjoyed a leisurely meal of fresh fruit with a local solicitor, Maître Hollert, who was a veteran of the French Revolutionary army. It's a breakfast that Napoleonic historians have never been able to digest.* Grouchy was by all accounts an excellent swordfighter and a brave cavalryman, very obedient when given precise orders, but when left to his own devices, he was lost. He had previously commanded cavalry units, but never a whole army. According to Dominique de Villepin, Grouchy 'lacked instinct, initiative and experience'. And yet here he was, sent off to face Blücher, a bloodthirsty warrior with fifty years of battle experience.

However, as all Bonapartist historians will tell you, this choice of unreliable commanders was less a case of bad

---

* Marcel Proust makes fun of Grouchy's inactivity in *A la Recherche du Temps Perdu*. In volume three, *Le Côté de Guermantes*, he has one of Grouchy's descendants arrive late for a society dinner. His furious wife humiliates him by snapping, 'I see that, even for minor things, being late is a tradition in your family.' A Proustian putdown – the ultimate condemnation for a famous French name.

judgement on Napoleon's part than a need to bow to circumstances. His most faithful officers were all dead. His young aide-de-camp Jean-Baptiste Muiron had died in Italy, taking a bullet that was meant for Napoleon. Louis Charles Desaix had fallen at the Battle of Marengo in 1800, shot through the heart while leading the victory charge. Louis-Alexandre Berthier, Napoleon's chief of staff, had died on 1 June, falling (or throwing himself) out of the window of his chateau, perhaps mortified for having become a royalist like all the others in 1814, and for refusing Napoleon's invitation to join him again.

The list of the faithful Napoleonic dead goes on: Marshal Jean Lannes, hit by a cannonball in 1809; Marshal Jean-Baptiste Bessières, also killed by a cannonball in Germany in 1813, of whom Napoleon later said, 'If I'd had Bessières at Waterloo, my Guard would have won the victory'; Marshal Michel Duroc, who also died in battle in Germany in 1813, such a valued aide-de-camp that he was known as 'Napoleon's shadow'.*

Meanwhile, his greatest cavalry officer, also incidentally his brother-in-law, Joachim Murat, had deserted him. Despite being allowed to marry Napoleon's sister Caroline and given the title of King of Naples, Murat had decided not to support Napoleon when the allies were closing in in 1814. On Napoleon's return in 1815 Murat had offered his support, but Napoleon refused, probably because he didn't like the

---

* Duroc was such a close companion that Napoleon later used his name as an alias when escaping from France (see Chapter 6).

man – he called him a 'vain cockerel'. The refusal was a mistake, because on the battlefield Murat was no chicken at all.

In short, Napoleon had no choice but to surround himself with untrustworthy men. Certainly the rank and file didn't trust their leaders – except their beloved Napoleon of course. In his memoirs, Sergeant Hippolyte de Mauduit accused the turncoat generals of being 'unworthy to command such troops. Some were traitors, making vows to prevent us from winning; others were soft, indecisive and lethargic, unwilling to attack.'

The ordinary soldiers were itching to fight and avenge the defeats of 1814, Mauduit stressed: 'The army itself was fully committed, everything about it suggested the greatest fighting spirit – at least among the soldiers and subalterns, because most of our generals and too many of our officers were tired of glory and no longer had the energy, the live-liness of mind and body, and the clear conscience that had earned them their brilliant military reputation.'

Napoleon was fully aware of this, but he somehow managed to convince himself that everything would be OK anyway. On the morning of 18 June he held a breakfast party in his lodgings at Le Caillou farm, using his own crockery, which had finally turned up on one of his personal luggage wagons – a favourable omen. He announced to his general staff that with Marshal Grouchy holding the Prussians at bay in the east, they would have plenty of time to beat the English.

Soult knew that Napoleon and Wellington had never met on the battlefield before, and that it might be dangerous to underestimate the Englishman who had chased the French army out of Spain. Soult himself had lost to Wellington in Toulouse in 1814, and expressed some scepticism about an easy victory at Waterloo – but this clearly wasn't the right time for doubts.

'Just because you have been defeated by Wellington, you think he is a great general,' Napoleon snapped, 'but I'm telling you he's a bad general, that the British are bad soldiers, and that it will be a picnic.'

General Antoine Drouot, in charge of the artillery, chipped in with his own negative thoughts: 'We can't fight this morning. The artillery will get bogged down.'

Marshal Honoré Reille, an infantry general, compounded the depressing mood: 'The English infantry is unbeatable because of its calm tenacity and superior accuracy. Before we can reach them with our bayonets, we must expect to lose half of our attacking soldiers.'

Napoleon's own brother Jérôme, who had served in Russia but been demoted because he was such an incompetent commander, proved that it had been a bad idea to invite him along by pronouncing gloomily that 'Here, we will find either our resurrection or our tomb.'*

In short, if Napoleon had hoped for a fluffy Belgian pancake type of breakfast with his commanders, he must

---

* Jérôme's morose mood was nothing new. On his way to Belgium, he had attended a country fête organised to whip up support for Napoleon, but had been unable to say anything positive or look anything but glum. A young French lieutenant called Le Sénécal noted in his memoirs that 'I saw his downcast attitude as the prelude to our imminent ruin'.

quickly have realised that he was in a room full of soggy waffles.

Despite all this negativity, before battle began at 11.30 a.m. (signalled by three blank cannon rounds), the French army was at its most magnificent. Lieutenant Jacques-François Martin described the scene vividly: 'The bayonets, helmets and breastplates were sparkling; the flags, the standards, the lancers' pennants all rippled with the three colours in the wind. The drums beat, the trumpets sounded, and the regiment's musicians gave us a rousing rendition of "Veillons au salut de l'Empire".'* In *Les Misérables*, Victor Hugo has Napoleon gazing at his army before Waterloo and exclaiming, 'Magnifique, magnifique!' To Hugo's readers, who knew what was about to happen, it was a moment of perfect pathos, a tableau of tragic heroes marching fearlessly to their death like gladiators hailing *l'Empereur* and proclaiming that 'we who are about to die salute you'.

General Etienne Lefol, who was struggling to get his cannons into place, was less poetic. He recalled in his memoirs the horror of moving guns around on the Belgian lanes where two battles had just been fought. The worst thing, he said, was 'the sound of the wheels crushing the skulls of soldiers whose brains and tattered flesh spread hideously across the road'. Battles, he knew, produced as much gore as they did glory. Lefol was consoled to hear the

---

* This was Napoleon's national anthem, and contained patriotic lines like 'the well-being of the universe depends on the well-being of our homeland, and if ever we are enslaved, all nations will be in chains'. Napoleon did not believe in modesty.

sound of crushed bone being drowned out by the voices of the surviving troops who were bellowing out a French marching tune, 'La Victoire est à nous' – victory is ours.

On the morning of 18 June 1815, this was somewhat premature, but Bonapartist historians have been trying to make it ring true ever since.

3

NAPOLEON DIDN'T LOSE THE BATTLE
(Everyone Else Did)

'Bataille terrible où la victoire, au milieu des armées confondues, se trompa d'étendard.'

'A terrible battle where, with all the armies intermingled, victory chose the wrong flag.'

– nineteenth-century French writer François-René de Chateaubriand

I

Things began to go wrong for Napoleon almost immediately. His cannons started to pound the English lines, but instead of bouncing and inflicting havoc, many of the cannonballs plopped harmlessly into the mud and stayed there.

Meanwhile, he ordered an attack on a farm called Hougoumont, halfway between the French and English lines, on the extreme left flank of the French army. However, in giving his order, Napoleon was acting on incomplete information. Earlier, he had sent out General François-Nicolas Haxo to report on possible allied fortifications along their front line. Haxo had omitted to mention that Hougoumont was more of a fortress than a farmhouse, with high brick walls around the farmyard, a thick wooden gate and a tower that was a perfect vantage point for snipers. Not only that, it was protected by a dense woodland that would prevent artillerymen dragging even the lightest cannons anywhere near the walls.

The farm was heavily manned by 1,700 highly trained British Guards and 300 Germans from one of the Nassau regiments, ensuring that the 30 metres of open ground between the woods and the walls of Hougoumont would be a killing field for any Frenchman who set foot in it.

All this shouldn't have mattered, though, because Napoleon's orders were simply to send out skirmishers and keep the farm's occupiers occupied, in the hope that they would call up reinforcements and weaken Wellington's centre.

As it was merely a tactical diversion, the job was given to Napoleon's brother Jérôme, who decided to launch an all-out attack. After his first assault had been repelled (almost killing Jérôme in the process, and mortally wounding another of Napoleon's few trusted generals, Pierre-François Bauduin), Jérôme decided to encircle the farm and even sent cavalry against the high brick walls. In all, throughout the day he would launch eight waves of men against the almost impregnable fortress, setting it alight and killing many of its defenders but wasting the lives of 8,000 Frenchmen in what was supposed to be a simple feint to distract Wellington.

Hougoumont did provide the French with some heroes, most notably Sous-lieutenant Legros ('Fatman'), a huge former sergeant who had come out of retirement to join Napoleon, and who ran at the farm's north gate with an axe and succeeded in forcing a breach, under furious fire from within. A few Frenchmen managed to get inside the farmyard full of firing, bayoneting Guardsmen, only to be massacred. The gate was re-closed, with Legros left lying just outside, the axe still in his hand.

Mostly, though, Hougoumont was about senseless slaughter. When British cannons joined the defence of the farm from afar, they began decimating the lines of Frenchmen waiting to attack. A young soldier called Larreguy de Civrieux was among them: 'Soon our feet were soaked in blood. In less than half an hour our ranks were more than halved. We all stood stoically awaiting death or terrible injury . . . No mortally wounded man gave his dying breath without expressing his devotion to the Emperor.' But they probably weren't shouting 'Vive Jérôme!'

Not that any of this was Napoleon's fault, according to his French admirers. Lacking competent marshals, he had no choice but to trust his young brother, and after all he had given Jérôme a very simple task that should have been within even his limited capabilities.

In *Les Misérables*, Victor Hugo seems to excuse the waste of lives by suggesting that Hougoumont was a vital strategic point on the battlefield. He ironises about 'a dung pit, a few hoes and spades, some carts, an old well with its iron wheel, a hopping foal, a jumping turkey . . . This is the farmyard that Napoleon dreamed of capturing . . . If he had managed to take this little patch of land, he might have won the world.'

The trouble was that there was a very large patch of land to the east that was still held by Wellington's men, who showed no sign of wanting to leave.

II

These days it is generally agreed that sending massed ranks of infantrymen marching in full view towards a well-armed enemy is rather heartless. We have all read about World War One soldiers climbing out of their trenches and immediately falling in their thousands to withering machine-gun fire. Machine guns didn't exist in 1815, but there were plenty of weapons deadly enough to wipe out whole lines of advancing men. The worst was probably the innocuous-sounding grapeshot,* a mass of grape-sized lumps of metal that could be fired from a cannon in a scatter-pattern, killing or mutilating far more efficiently than a single cannonball. Grapeshot was often augmented with chains, nails and any odd bits of shrapnel that were handy – when firing hot metal at short range at an enemy, it was important to maim as many bodies as possible.

This deadly hailstorm, as well as straightforward cannon-balls, was what Napoleon's infantry now faced as he sent

---

* The French, for once, are less romantic when naming something. Their word for grapeshot is *mitraille*, a descriptive term for a collection of metal projectiles, the '-*aille*' suffix giving the word negative, random overtones (*ferraille*, for example, is odd bits of *fer*, or iron). *Mitraille* really does conjure up an ugly spray of metal.

them marching towards the centre of Wellington's line. And that was before they came in range of the muskets awaiting them on the top of the ridge.

There has been much criticism of Napoleon's full-frontal assault, especially because the soldiers were made to advance in densely packed columns, 200 men wide and twenty-four rows deep, so that they were much easier to mow down with cannon and grapeshot than a wider line. Some French historians try to explain the attack by alleging that Napoleon's orders were misinterpreted, but Napoleon himself had always shown that he saw no moral problem with sending large numbers of men to an almost certain death, if it meant winning the day. In 1813 he had warned the Austrian negotiator Metternich that he was willing to take huge casualties to defend France (and his own throne, of course): 'A man like me cares little about the lives of a million men.' Napoleon had also told parliament that 'Any man who values his own life more than national glory and the esteem of his comrades has no place in the French army.' In other words, you're cannon fodder and you'd better enjoy it.

At about 1.30 p.m., Napoleon therefore sent about 16,000 men on a one-kilometre walk across the muddy fields of soaked rye, with English cannons scything through the ranks as if harvesting the cereals. The soldiers marched valiantly on, terrifying a front line of Belgo-Dutch troops, who scattered before them. Thinking they had broken the English defences, the French began to cheer, and charged forward. But there was a line of British troops on the ridge, and they unleashed a volley of musket fire at almost point-blank range. The surviving French infantrymen decided they had had enough and began to dash back towards their lines.

This was where Sir William Ponsonby and Lord Uxbridge famously led the British cavalry charging heroically down-hill, trampling the fleeing infantrymen, and galloping so far forward that they ran into a superior force of better-armed French horsemen who cut them to shreds. Wellington's infantry, on the other hand, stoically held their line at the top of the ridge, waiting for Napoleon's next move.

Fortunately for Wellington's infantry, and unfortunately for both Napoleon and Bonapartist historians, the next attack was led by Napoleon's loosest cannon – Ney.

Ney saw a column of men moving away from the battle-field on the allied side, and for some reason decided that the British were retreating, even though the heavy fire coming from the ridge should have convinced him other-wise. Ney therefore ordered the French cavalry to charge. General Delort answered that he couldn't attack without Napoleon's direct order, but Ney overrode him (if that is not a bad cavalry-related pun), and 5,000 men and horses began their characteristic French trot towards the British infantry line that was still standing unbroken, formed into defensive squares, and defended by a battery of cannons.

The French cavalry were an impressive sight – a British artillery officer, Captain Alexander Cavalié Mercer, recalled with typical English restraint that 'These grenadiers & cheval were very fine troops, clothed in blue uniforms without facings, cuffs, or collars. Broad, very broad buff belts, and huge muff caps, made them appear gigantic fellows.' Not that this prevented Mercer and his comrades from trying to destroy the colourful tableau.

When the horses were little more than 50 yards away, the British cannons opened fire. Mercer remembered that 'the discharge of every gun was followed by a fall of men and horses like that of grass before the mower's scythe'. He saw Ney at the head of the charge: 'An officer in a rich uniform, his breast covered with decorations, whose earnest gesticulations were strangely contrasted with the solemn demeanour of those to whom they were addressed.'

A few brave French horsemen broke through, but could only fire a pistol shot or throw a lance into the British squares. Some even leaped over the front line of troops,* but their horses were disembowelled as they passed, and the unsaddled cavalrymen were mostly bayoneted as they lay helplessly on the ground, surrounded by English infantry. Men whose horses had been shot tried to run away on foot – a humiliating spectacle, as many were caught by light-footed skirmishers. It was Agincourt all over again – the flower of French knighthood slaughtered in the mud by nimble common soldiers.

As his men and their chargers fell, Ney himself had several horses shot from under him, but he urged the cavalry on to death or glory. Captain Mercer heard 'the now loud and rapid vociferations of him who had led them on and remained unhurt'. At one point, Ney was seen slashing at an abandoned cannon with his broken sword, waiting for a

* The image of horses leaping over the line of bayonet-wielding soldiers after crossing a kilometre or more of muddy field occurs more often in heroism-seeking French accounts than pragmatic British versions.

new horse so that he could charge the English again. His own survival was little short of miraculous.

Perhaps it is because Ney survived the charge that French historians – including Napoleon – are so merciless with him. Most of them explain that Napoleon only gave general orders to his commanders, trusting them to deal with the details, so that he was horrified to see Ney sending cavalry forward without infantry or artillery support, and exclaimed that 'he [Ney] is compromising the destiny of France'.

Ney's recklessness forced Napoleon to follow suit, explaining to Soult that 'Ney has turned a sure thing into an uncertainty, but now the movement has begun, the only thing to do is support it.' Napoleon felt obliged to launch another, even more massive, cavalry attack, one that at least had a chance of breaking through.

Ney continued to lead the charges with suicidal determination, and wave after wave of cavalry ran at the tightly packed British squares. Victor Hugo described the carnage poetically in *Les Misérables*: 'Each square was like a volcano attacked by a cloud.' And sure enough, the clouds were thinning fast.

All in all, Ney might as well have had the horses butchered and served up for lunch.* The Bonapartist historian Jean-Claude Damamme heaps infamy on Ney by describing the animal abuse in bloody detail. He depicts a wounded *chasseur* begging a surgeon to look after his horse, which is standing nearby, its entrails hanging down into the mud. It is Bijou

---

* It is of course ironic that the man responsible for so many horses' deaths had a name that was pronounced 'neigh'.

('Jewel'), the trusty mount that has seen the cavalryman through every campaign since the Battle of the Pyramids in 1798. As the surgeon looks on, another cannonball flashes by and finishes off Bijou. A brave veteran's career has been ended by Ney.

Another man, a dragoon, makes it back to the French lines, having left behind the body of his horse, Cadet. Damamme lists its impressive military record – Prussia and Poland 1806–7, Spain 1808, Austria 1809, a return to Spain 1810–11, Russia 1812, Saxony 1813. The old horse was almost a living history of Napoleon's expanding empire – the only thing old Cadet seems to have missed was the birth of the Emperor's baby boy. And now it was tear-jerkingly dead.

Most people agree that Ney was suffering from a death-wish. He was a veteran of some seventy battles, he had been through the horrors of the Russian winter, turned traitor in 1814, taken up Napoleon's cause again in 1815, and now saw that the whole epic story was coming to an end. Two days before Waterloo, he was heard saying, 'Oh how I wish those English cannonballs could all hit me in the guts.'

The reason for this deathwish becomes clear when you hear what he told another marshal, Jean-Baptiste d'Erlon, during the battle: 'You and I have to perish here, because if the English grapeshot doesn't do for us, we're going to be hanged.'

As it happened, both would survive the battle. Erlon escaped to Germany, and opened a brasserie near Munich. But Ney foretold his own future more accurately. Charged with treason by Louis XVIII's victorious government, he was shot by firing squad in Paris in December 1815. Typically, he refused a blindfold and ordered the firing squad to 'fire, my comrades, and aim well'. Despite his bad performance at Waterloo, he died a hero in French eyes, but only because he went on to become a victim of Louis XVIII's royalists, who are regarded by almost every French historian, even those who blame Ney for the defeat at Waterloo, as some of the biggest villains in their country's history.

Even then, Ney doesn't get *all* of the blame for this waste of cavalrymen and horses. According to Victor Hugo, the terrain chosen by Wellington had one last secret to reveal. As the brave French horsemen rode towards the English lines, they suddenly discovered a hidden line of natural defence – a sunken lane blocking their way like some huge inhuman obstacle at the Grand National. Hugo describes the charging cavalry suddenly being tipped headlong into a ditch that soon turned into a mass grave: 'Riders and horses rolled over, crushing one another, turning the chasm into a mass of flesh, and when the ditch was full of survivors, others trod on them . . . This began the end of the battle.'

This 'ravine of death' looms large in the 1970 film *Waterloo*, directed by the Russian Sergei Bondarchuk, in which Rod Steiger plays Napoleon, Christopher Plummer Wellington and Orson Welles a hideous Louis XVIII. The film shows French horses tumbling into a hole that is more like a small quarry than a country lane. It's so deep that nowadays, the film scene – like most of Bondarchuk's footage of horses falling – would be banned for cruelty to animals.

But in fact the sunken lane seems to have been an invention, or an elaboration, on Hugo's part, because the charging

British cavalry had crossed it easily, and early visitors to the battlefield described little more than a depression with relatively shallow sides and no hedges to hide it from advancing horses. Hugo seems to have needed his 'ravine of death' to underline his central point: with both Ney and God in league to ensure poor Napoleon's defeat, what hope did he have?

III

Another enemy now appeared in Napoleon's telescope as he turned it to the east. What he had originally taken for Grouchy's French troops finally arriving to support him turned out to be Prussians.

Napoleon's fears about Grouchy were proving to be grounded. After his strawberry breakfast, the marshal had gone off on a riding tour of eastern Belgium – what one French historian called 'une promenade militaire', vainly searching for Prussians and ignoring the pleas of his subalterns to obey the first rule of Napoleonic battle and 'march to the cannon' – that is, go to Napoleon's aid as soon as they heard the battle starting over at Waterloo.

When they heard the first artillery barrage, some of Grouchy's officers reminded him of this rule. They were about four hours' march away, so there was still time to be useful (Napoleon calculated that one of his battles usually lasted about six hours). French historians have noted the words used to Grouchy by Etienne-Maurice Gérard, a veteran of Austerlitz, who had distinguished himself at Ligny: 'Monsieur le Maréchal, our duty is to march to the cannon. When

Wellington is beaten, we will still have time to sort out Blücher.' Grouchy reportedly got irritated and objected that they would march too slowly because of the bad conditions underfoot, at which point Gérard lost his temper: '*Sacré nom de Dieu!* Events command you to advance and you're not moving faster than a mussel.'* Offended, Grouchy ordered them to march the men further away from Waterloo, towards Wavre, and into the arms of French historians who delight in rubbishing his reputation. The nineteenth-century writer Achille Tenaille de Vaulabelle is withering about Grouchy: 'With more decision and action, and with a keener appreciation of warfare and his position as an army commander, Marshal Grouchy could have transformed the disaster of Waterloo into a great victory. It was his duty to do so. He did not do it.'

Napoleon himself poured all the irony he could muster on Grouchy when discussing the battle with his companion on Saint Helena, Emmanuel de Las Cases: 'Marshal Grouchy, with 34,000 men and 108 cannons, managed to find the secret, which seemed impossible to find, of how to avoid being either on the battlefield at Mont Saint Jean, or at Wavre on the 18th.'

Napoleon was all the more furious, both on the day and in hindsight, because he had dictated an order to Grouchy at six in the morning on the 18th: 'You must manoeuvre in our direction and try to join our army before any Prussian troops move between us.' Marshal Soult had added his own

---

* This was not a pun on 'not moving a muscle', because the French for mussel is *moule*. Mussels, of course, stay clamped to their rocks.

message to the order: 'Don't waste a moment before moving towards us.'

However, this is where Soult takes flak from Bonapartist historians. He had just one job – to make sure Napoleon's orders were delivered – and he messed it up by entrusting the order to Grouchy to only two messengers. One of them got lost, and the other vanished without trace, probably after stumbling across some Prussians. When Grouchy failed to appear at Waterloo, Napoleon asked Soult how many messengers he had sent, and, hearing the answer, groaned, 'Berthier would have sent a hundred!' Berthier was, of course, his recently deceased former chief of staff.

At about 5.30 p.m. Napoleon was able to remind Ney that his original orders that morning had not been to charge blindly at cannons; his mission had been to capture a farm in front of the British centre, at La Haye Sainte ('the sacred hedge').

Infantrymen, furious at being left behind while the cavalry got massacred – the veterans knew that Napoleon's plans usually involved a mass attack of cavalry supported by infantry – were sent in and overran the farm quickly. Ney realised that from the protection of the farmyard walls, French artillery could rake the English front line with deadly cannon fire. (French accounts of this realisation have a strong undertone of 'duh!'.) Ney began to do just that, and the English centre suddenly started to weaken, as Napoleon had known it would.

This is supposedly when Wellington saw what was happening and uttered his prayer 'give me night or give me Blücher'. Though other accounts have him predicting simply that 'either night or Blücher will come', implying that he never doubted victory, or at the very least expected a stale-mate.

The French infantry captain Jean Baptiste Lemonnier-Delafosse described Wellington's despair at around 5.30 p.m. In his *Souvenirs Militaires*, the fervent Bonapartist quoted a letter that he received a few years after the battle from one of Wellington's aides-de-camp, identified only as Monsieur Hamilton,* in what reads like a decidedly un-Iron Duke-like state of panic: 'Lord Wellington, bare-headed, was leaning against a tree, motionlessly watching his defeated army . . . They were fleeing all around him . . . I saw tears in his eyes . . . The poor lord was a pitiful sight – he was no longer a man. Plunged in despairing thoughts, he was a statue of stupor. Suddenly, we heard cannon fire on our left, from the direction of Wavre. He lifted his head, listened, and cried: "The Prussian cannons. We're saved!" And the man, the general, re-emerged. He rallied, etc. And you know what happened after that . . .'

Lemonnier-Delafosse added that 'Monsieur Hamilton's pen was restrained by patriotism, but saying that much is enough to show that Wellington was beaten before the Prussians arrived.' The French captain concluded that Wellington's success 'in Belgium' (Lemonnier-Delafosse finds it hard to pronounce the name 'Waterloo', and calls the battle 'Mont Saint Jean') was due to 'the elements first of

---

* Possibly Major Andrew Hamilton, ADC to Major General Sir Edward Barnes.

all, and to Marshal Ney's unthinking bravery. Moreover, no strategist has ever approved of the English army's position.'

The words 'sour grapeshot' come to mind.

IV

Meanwhile, with the British reeling, Ney spotted another opportunity to show what Lemonnier-Delafosse diplomatically called his 'unthinking bravery'. Chomping at the bit to launch another assault, Ney sent his aide-de-camp, Colonel Heymès, to Napoleon for more troops, apparently having forgotten already that he himself had sent thousands of them to a wasteful, senseless death.

Predictably, Napoleon was incensed: 'Troops? Where do you want me to get them? Do you want me to create them?' He did still have one card up his sleeve (or rather in his waistcoat), but it was his most precious one, the ace that he never liked to play unless it was sure to win – his *Garde Impériale*.

In past battle reports, Napoleon had often written that 'la Garde a donné' – 'the Guards performed', a succinct phrase indicating that his elite troops had swiftly and efficiently finished the job of routing the enemy. Now, though, it would be more of a desperate move. The enemy line was shaken, but not yet on the verge of breaking. Sending in the *Garde* would not be the *coup de grâce* that it usually was. It would be his final trump, and he would have to hope that Wellington had no riposte.

But with Blücher's Prussians beginning to arrive in increasing numbers, Napoleon had no choice. He had to wipe out the effects of Grouchy's inactivity and Ney's madness by sending in his coolest, best-trained troops.

Napoleon rode his horse over to the 5,000-strong *Vieille Garde*, who were, as usual, stationed close to his command post.

'My friends,' he told them, 'you are at the *moment suprême*. Your job is not to shoot. You must engage the enemy in hand-to-hand combat, and, at the point of your bayonet, throw him back into the ravine from where he came, and from where he threatens France and the Empire.'

This was all in a day's work for the Old Guard, who naturally replied with hearty shouts of 'Vive l'Empereur!'

But yet again, Napoleon was let down. A traitor, named and shamed by French historians as Capitaine du Barrail, rode towards English lines, shouting 'Vive le Roi!' so that he wouldn't be shot, and informed the enemy that the *Garde Impériale* were about to attack, led by Napoleon himself. The British knew that this would be the final, all-or-nothing French charge, and had time to brace themselves for one last onslaught. Accordingly, Wellington closed up his line and positioned cavalry at the point where the *Garde* were expected. Yet again, the Brits and their treacherous friends were cheating.

After a forty-five-minute cannon barrage, the first wave of the *Garde* saluted Napoleon and set off – 2,900 men in three tight lines, marching slowly, impassively, as if on parade, grouped around their eagle standards, their muskets on their shoulders, red plumes proudly fluttering from their tall busbies.

French accounts of the *Garde*'s march towards the English lines – effectively the last great French attack of the

Napoleonic Wars – ooze with tragic hindsight. Dominique de Villepin calls it a 'terrible moment where action became sublime thanks to the sacrifice of the immortals'. Victor Hugo declared that 'history has nothing more moving than these last death throes'. Jean-Claude Damamme reminds us that these men had been 'the victors of Europe'.

Unfortunately for these 'immortal' heroes, they were being led into battle by a mortal with a deathwish – Ney. When his horse was again shot from under him, he simply continued on foot. As he and his troops came closer to the top of the ridge, the drumbeat quickened and the *Garde* marched faster, while maintaining their impassive, machine-like advance.

Then came the British welcome. Cannons ripped into the *Garde* from front and side. Men fell in whole rows, sending muskets, busbies and limbs flying everywhere. About 500 were killed by the first salvo, but they simply closed ranks and marched on. Suddenly, Wellington unleashed his secret weapon: 2,000 Guardsmen lying down in four rows, hidden in a wheatfield. He gave his famous order: 'Up, Guards! Make ready! Fire!' And the British did just that, at a range of twenty paces. Even with primitive muskets, no one could miss.

This shock, coupled with a sudden English charge with fixed bayonets and the emergence of Hanoverian troops from Hougoumont who began firing at the *Garde*'s rear, was enough, and at this point some French historians face up to the painful task of admitting the inadmissible. Dominique de Villepin recognises that 'the impossible happened: the *Garde* retreated'. (Note that they didn't turn and run, they just retreated.)

Others refuse to countenance this national tragedy.

General Antoine Drouot later claimed that 'The large number of wounded men who left the battlefield made people believe that the *Garde* had been routed.' Another veteran, Captain Duthilt, agreed, stressing that 'Except for the Old Guard, everyone began to run.'

In an instant, with the *Garde* (apparently) doing the unthinkable, the French will to fight suddenly broke. General Drouot explained that 'a panicking terror transmitted itself to the adjacent groups of men who hurriedly began to flee'.

By all accounts, once they decided they had had enough, the majority of French soldiers didn't hang around to explain why. Shouting 'Sauve qui peut!' ('Every man for himself!'), they began to disappear at speed into the deepening gloom, abandoning weapons, baggage, and the few officers who tried to rally them.

Sensing victory, Wellington appeared on the ridge and waved his hat, the order for the whole front line to advance and fulfil the role that Napoleon's *Garde* had always performed.

As Jean-Claude Damamme describes the victorious troops charging down the ridge, he tries to minimise Wellington's great moment by stressing that his soldiers weren't all British. Everyone was ganging up on Napoleon, he says: 'English, Scots, Irish, Belgians, Dutch, Brunswickians, Nassauers, Hanoverians, Westphalians, Prussians, all combining their weapons and their flags. It was a fight to the death of the multitude against just one nation. Just one man.' Anything to dampen the flames of British triumphalism.

Napoleon saw what was happening, but all French sources maintain that he stood his ground, even though he was dangerously close to the fighting. He personally took command of the artillery, and continued to pound the British lines. When the rout became unstoppable, he tried to join the *Garde* to make a stand. His officers had to drag him away, one of them, Captain Coignet, asking, 'What are you doing? Isn't a victory enough for them?'

Meanwhile, Marshal Ney was still out there, trying to commit suicide. On foot, his sword broken, his uniform torn and bloodied, he came across a group of 800 infantrymen who had been held in reserve, and were still in good order, hoping to join up with the rest of the French army and regroup, or to dig in and protect the retreat. Their commander, General Durutte, went off to reconnoitre, at which point Ney ordered the men to charge the British lines. They naturally obeyed, only to run into a force of English cavalry who cut the isolated Frenchmen to pieces.

In *Les Misérables*, Hugo describes the scene, with Ney 'sweating, fire in his eyes, froth on his lips, his jacket unbuttoned, one of his epaulettes half-severed by a Horse Guard's sabre, his eagle badge dented by a bullet, bloody, muddy, magnificent, a broken sword in his fist, he was saying: "Come and see how a Marshal of France dies on the battlefield!" But in vain. He didn't die.'

It really wasn't Ney's day.

V

At least some of the *Garde* had held fast and were withdrawing in tight formation. One battalion of 550 men has gone down in legend thanks to their last stand. Refusing to join the general flight, they formed into a square, and resisted the attacks of the British troops swarming around them. When a hundred of them were killed by a single cannon salvo, they simply closed ranks and continued to fight.

Their commander was General Pierre Cambronne, who had been the head of Napoleon's personal guard during the exile on Elba. Called on to surrender, Cambronne famously answered, 'The *Garde* dies but never surrenders.' His brave retort was reported in the *Journal Général de France* on 24 June 1815, and widely re-quoted throughout the country.

When the British tried to persuade him that the battle was over, Cambronne defiantly shouted 'Merde!' – a moment in French history so famous that *merde* is euphemistically known as *le mot de Cambronne*, or 'Cambronne's word'.

Faced with such courage, the British sportingly withdrew the line of cannons pointed at the *Garde*, and left them to claim that they, at least, had won a corner of a foreign field that would forever be French. Well, no of course they didn't do that at all – the British cannons opened fire at point-blank range and allowed the *Garde* to keep its word, and die.

Cambronne himself was only wounded, and survived to deny at least part of the story about him. According to Jean-Claude Carrière's *Dictionnaire des Révélations Historiques et Contemporaines*, Cambronne later quipped, 'I couldn't have said "the *Garde* dies but never surrenders" because I'm not dead and I didn't surrender.'

Despite the heroism of a few hundred *Gardes*, the defeat was total, and as darkness fell, this part of Belgium was overrun by French soldiers fleeing for their lives. Lemonnier-Delafosse, Marshal Foy's aide-de-camp, called the scene a 'hideous spectacle. A torrent pouring down a mountainside, uprooting everything before it, is a weak image to describe the mass of men, horses and carriages crushing each other.'

In his diaries, Captain Coignet remembered the chaotic scenes in Genappe, 7 kilometres south of the battlefield: 'Soldiers of every regiment . . . were marching with no order at all, confused, knocking into each other, squeezing through the streets of this small town, fleeing the Prussian cavalry. Nothing could calm them . . . they would listen to no one. Cavalrymen were blowing their horse's brains out, infantrymen were blowing out their own so as not to fall into enemy hands.'

The Prussians, frustrated at missing most of the battle, and virulently anti-French because of the invasions they had suffered, were taking no prisoners. Blücher had told his men that he would personally kill any soldier who brought him a French captive. French accounts of the aftermath of the battle are full of Prussian atrocities. Not only were wounded combatants robbed and finished off where they lay, unarmed French wagon drivers were massacred. At Le Caillou farm, Napoleon's billet the previous night, which had been turned into a hospital caring for the wounded of all sides, the Prussians removed all non-French soldiers from the barn and set fire to the building. Reading French history books, it is easy to understand the birth of an anti-Prussian hatred that would not be appeased until after 1918, or even 1945.

Meanwhile, the Bonapartist historians tell us, the unde-serving victor Wellington was able to meet up with his saviour, Blücher, in one of the biggest anti-climaxes in military history. Blücher couldn't speak English, so he greeted Wellington with 'mein lieber Kamerad', and then, not knowing what else to say, added in French: 'Quelle affaire!' Not exactly Molière-like repartee. Napoleon would certainly have provided history with a decent quote.

According to Jean-Claude Damamme, Wellington was looking anything but jubilant. He quotes an unidentified British officer as saying that the Duke looked 'abattu', down-cast – although *abattu* can also mean shot down or butchered, and comes from the French root word *battu*, meaning beaten. It's all heavy, subliminal stuff.

Napoleon was already on his way back to France, and was seen at Quatre-Bras (the vital crossroads where Ney had dithered two days earlier), his arms folded, weeping at the sheer unfairness of it all. He had returned from Elba to save France from a corrupt and spineless king; he had offered Europe lasting peace and been rejected; and then, despite a severe attack of urinary disease, syphilis and/or piles, he had bumped across half of France and Belgium to execute a daring battle plan that would have paid off if God, the weather and a gaggle of incompetent or treacherous French commanders hadn't each put a spoke in his cannon wheels.

Non, he had not won his great gamble, but then, as various French commentators – including Napoleon himself – have explained, it really wasn't his fault. And now it was time for a new battle to begin – the fight to rewrite history.

4

'MERDE' TO WELLINGTON,
THE LOSER

'L'ennemi fut contenu, fut repoussé et recula; il avait épuisé
ses forces et l'on n'en avait plus rien à craindre.'
'The enemy was contained, was pushed back, and retreated;
they were exhausted, and we had nothing left to fear.'
 – Napoleon, writing about Wellington's army in his report
immediately after Waterloo

'Ce ne fut pas lord Wellington qui vainquit; sa défense fut
opiniâtre, admirable d'énergie, mais il fut forcé, battu.'
'It wasn't Lord Wellington who won; his defence was stubborn,
and admirably energetic, but he was pushed back and beaten.'
 – Captain Marie Jean Baptiste Lemonnier-Delafosse, in his
Souvenirs Militaires

I

In the first edition of one of France's best-known encyclopedias, the *Nouveau Larousse Illustré*, published in seven volumes between 1897 and 1904, there is a surprisingly poetic entry on Waterloo. The battle is defined as 'the last conflict of the epic Napoleonic era, fought on 18 June 1815, in the small valley which separates the plateau of Mont-Saint-Jean-Waterloo, occupied by Wellington's English forces, from the hillock of Resomme or Belle-Alliance, where the French army was camped.' The battle is not defined more simply and encyclopedically, as, for example, 'the defeat of Napoleon Bonaparte and his French army by the British and the Prussians'. It is just, for some unexplained reason, the last battle of the Napoleonic era.

The sense of French revisionism about whether Waterloo actually was a defeat is reminiscent of the pitch for the Hollywood idiot movie *Bill and Ted's Excellent Adventure*: 'History is about to be rewritten . . . by two guys who can't spell.'

In the case of Waterloo, history has definitely been rewritten, or overwritten. If you ask a French person about 18 June – 'le dix-huit juin' – they almost certainly won't think that you are referring to 1815 and Waterloo. They will cite De Gaulle's *Appel du dix-huit juin*, the Général's famous radio appeal from London in 1940 for Frenchmen to cross the Channel and join him in the struggle to liberate France. Hardly any Frenchmen did so, resulting in the fact that only 177 French troops landed in Normandy on

D-Day,* but the date of the *Appel du dix-huit juin* has been implanted in the French folk memory (helped along by their history teachers), expunging Waterloo from the calendar.

However, among those French people who more readily associate 18 June with Waterloo, there is a real feeling that it was not a defeat, and that it was in some ways a great victory. To a British reader raised on images of brave redcoats winning eternal glory for themselves and their regiment, this may seem bizarre. But Bonapartist historians have had two centuries to fine-tune their version of the battle, and have come up with some forceful arguments.

They often quote, for example, the fact that France won the battle of the standard captures – French troops snatched at least four British regiments' flags (some say it was six), and lost only two of their Napoleonic eagles. In those almost medieval times of honour and glory, this was an important statistic.

More significantly, though, many French writers – including Napoleon – claim that the French army won the battle *against Wellington*. We saw earlier how Napoleon liked to divide campaigns into smaller episodes so that he could claim to have won more battles. Here, Bonapartist historians and veterans of Napoleon's army divide Waterloo itself into two parts – a victory against the British, followed by a defeat once the Prussians arrived. In any case, a partial triumph.

General Foy claimed that on 18 June Wellington was

---

* For a more detailed explanation, see my book *1000 Years of Annoying the French*.

'beaten from midday to six o'clock'. Captain Lemonnier-Delafosse called Waterloo an 'extraordinary battle, the only one in which there were two losers: first the English, then the French'.

Napoleon punctuates his own account of the day's action, composed on 20 June, with a paragraph claiming that in mid-afternoon 'the battle was won; we were occupying all the positions that the enemy had occupied at the start of the battle' (which was, of course, a lie). 'Marshal Grouchy, having assessed the movement of the Prussian army, was pursuing them, thereby assuring us of a great victory the following day. After eight hours of firing and infantry and cavalry charges, the whole army was able to look with satisfaction upon a battle won and the battlefield in our possession.' What happened immediately afterwards seems to be of secondary importance.

French historians are also fond of quoting Wellington's own admission in his report published in *The Times* on 22 June that he would have been lost without the Prussians: 'I should not do justice to my feelings or to Marshal Blücher and the Prussian army, if I do not attribute the successful result of this arduous day, to the cordial and timely assistance I received from them.' It sounds as though the Prussians had helped him put up a marquee for his birthday party, but to the French the meaning is clear – Napoleon had the Englishman pinned to the ropes and rocking back on his heels before a third boxer jumped into the ring.

A French Hussar by the name of Victor Dupuy confirmed this in his *Souvenirs Militaires*: 'The events of that deplorable day could so easily have been different . . . The English army was in disarray when the Prussians, who had evaded Marshal Grouchy, arrived on the battlefield and stole the victory that the English had more than lost. Without this . . . Waterloo Bridge would have been built across the Seine. At the very least, the bridge ought to have a statue of the Prussian general.'

The consensus among Bonapartist historians is simple: the British lost their part of the battle, and didn't deserve to share the victory.

These historians pour scorn on the British troops, who unlike Napoleon's fiercely devoted Guards were, as one French historian puts it, 'in uniform thanks to nothing but poverty or unemployment. In their ranks one frequented all sections of society, including the worst.' (He seems to be forgetting the huge numbers of men from all over the French empire conscripted into service by Napoleon to replace the hundreds of thousands of troops he lost in Russia.)

Both the French and the British often misquote Wellington as having nothing but upper-class English disdain for his own ordinary soldiers, whom he famously called 'the scum of the earth'. On the other hand, it is well known that Wellington admired the French army: 'They were excellent troops; I never on any occasion knew them to behave other than well. Their officers too were as good as possible.'

In fact, though, when Wellington branded his own troops 'scum' on 4 November 1813, he was saying something more subtle, albeit equally snobbish: 'A French army is composed very differently from ours. The conscription calls out a share

99

of every class – no matter whether your son or my son – all must march; but our friends – I may say it in this room – are the very scum of the earth. People talk of their enlisting from their fine military feeling – all stuff – no such thing. Some of our men enlist from having got bastard children – some for minor offences – many more for drink; but you can hardly conceive such a set brought together, and it really is wonderful that we should have made them the fine fellows they are.'

The French Bonapartist Jean-Claude Damamme goes further and besmirches the character of the British officers, clearly wanting to underline the notion that they were unworthy to be remembered as glorious victors. In Brussels before the battle, he says, kind-hearted Belgian girls gave their hearts to the visiting young bucks ('these beardless warriors'), but 'one is forced to note that these idylls were temporary, and the abandoned were legion'. One can only assume that French officers on campaign always married local girls before sleeping with them, and then took them home to meet *maman*.

Damamme also pokes fun at British officers vainly trying to introduce fox-hunting into Belgium, and coming up against furry resistance fighters: 'the hardy Belgian foxes refused to run from hounds launched in pursuit of their red pelt'.

The only British soldiers who gain any real respect from Bonapartists are the Scots (Auld Alliance *oblige*, of course). They were, one historian says, 'lively, friendly fellows, whose "skirts" flapped around their muscular calves, titillating the curiosity of the feminine population'.

But if Bonapartist historians find the Brits laughable, the Prussians were just plain, well, Prussian. The French-speaking Belgians called them *la vermine verte* – because of their green uniforms, not their politics. They stole cattle and poultry, they raped and pillaged, and killed anyone who tried to stop them, forcing Belgians to take to the woods. They requisitioned every available cart to transport their booty, and any mayor who failed to hand over his entire town as a billet was beaten up and jailed.

This abuse had been going on, we are told, ever since the Russians and Prussians 'liberated' Belgium from Napoleonic rule in 1814, inspired mainly by the psychotic French-hater Blücher. He had been captured by Napoleon's men at Lübeck in 1806 (he was later exchanged for a French marshal), and was out for revenge.

Blücher is often compared and contrasted with the noble, chivalrous French officers (until, of course, they went AWOL at Waterloo). He was known for sending his men rashly into battle – his nickname was Marshal Vorwärts (which would also have been a good name for France's Marshal Ney on 18 June) – and he is mocked for failing to grasp the strategy of war. With a startling lack of insight, he had written home to his wife from Belgium that 'we might stay here another year – Napoleon won't attack'.

Bonapartists are also keen to point out that at the end of his life, Blücher went totally mad and believed that he had been impregnated by an elephant and that the French had lit a fire under his floor so that he had to walk on tiptoes. They often ignore the fact that Blücher was almost offhand in his bravery. After the Battle of Lützen in 1813, he wrote to his wife: 'I was shot in the back. I'll bring the bullet home for you.'

In fact, according to the Bonapartists, not only was Wellington cheating because he had help from this mad old Francophobe and his barbarous Prussian troops, the British army wasn't even British. There were only 25,000 or so British soldiers in Wellington's army of 67,000 men. A recent issue of the (normally unbiased) magazine *L'Histoire* even implied that 'Wellington's troops were so diverse that there were several accidental but deadly clashes between friendly soldiers, especially when the Prussian reinforcements began to arrive at around 4 p.m.'

The implication is clear – the French army was pure, while the allies were watered down, incompetent and border-line insane.

II

Even if they concede that France ultimately lost possession of the battlefield, many French commentators still maintain that they won the *moral* victory. The key word here is *gloire* – glory. It is a term that crops up endlessly in French accounts of Waterloo, and Napoleon's career in general. Napoleon himself said that Waterloo was 'glorious, even if it was fatal for the French army'.

He is not the only Frenchman who fails to see the inherent contradiction in this idea. In a French dictionary of battles published in 1818, the authors said of Waterloo that 'both sides showed how far courage can go when one is fighting for national honour; but the French rose far above their enemies; at first victorious, then defeated by the most extraordinary change of fortune, they were greater, and acquired more glory from this setback than if victory had not evaded them'.

Similarly, in the introduction to his book *Histoire de la Campagne de 1815 – Waterloo*, the nineteenth-century historian Jean-Baptiste-Adolphe Charras, who was no fan of Napoleon, wrote that 'After reading this book, one man [Napoleon] might seem diminished; but on the other hand, the French army will seem grander, and France less bowed.'

In fact, 18 June 1815, we are meant to believe, was a day marked more than anything else by the death-defying bravery of the French soldier. This doesn't mean the suicidal rashness of Ney, repeatedly charging in the hope of taking a bullet and ending his career with a splash (of his own blood), but the stoic courage of the French soldier fighting for his country and his Emperor even when all the odds were stacked against him.

The French soldiers' bravery was all the more admirable, Bonapartists insist, because Napoleon's army at Waterloo had been hurriedly assembled to meet the combined might of the coalition.

Napoleon had not been able to boost numbers with conscripts – King Louis XVIII had abolished conscription, much to the relief of most Frenchmen and their families. And in the past he had been able to round up troops from other countries in his empire, but this too was now impossible. To compensate, Napoleon brought as many French veterans as possible out of retirement. France's navy had been decommissioned (the Brits wanted Britannia to rule the waves totally unchallenged), so sailors were transferred into the army, as were customs officers and forest wardens. And Napoleon also called for 'volunteers', though the notion of volunteering was a typically Napoleonic one – in Corrèze, an apple-growing area where it rains quite a lot, villages that produced too few volunteers had their trees cut down and their roof tiles removed.

In this way, between March and June 1815 Napoleon raised an astonishing new force of 413,000 men whom he stationed all over the country to guard against invaders. He also set about his personal arms race, mobilising public and private weapons factories to manufacture 40,000 rifles a month (this in a pre-production line age of wooden stocks, hand-forged barrels and individually cut flints), with a peak in June 1815 of 1,500 guns per day. The *cartoucherie* (cartridge factory) at the Château de Vincennes on the outskirts of Paris produced an amazing twelve million cartridges in two months.

Forts were repaired and armed with cannons, as were Paris's walls. The Old Guard even came to Paris to motivate the workers on the fortifications by playing rousing military music (though this might also have been a tactic to scare Parisian workers into action).

All in all, Napoleon's new army was a hurriedly raised, scantly trained force, united almost entirely by their determination to defend France and their Emperor (and, in some cases, their apple trees). This might explain their willingness to run away at the end of Waterloo when they saw the elite

Garde falter, but it also imbues them, in French eyes, with a kind of Dunkirk spirit, a refusal to let their country be invaded by the imperious foreigners. Morally, in Bonapartist eyes, they soar above the band of mercenaries paid for by the English enemy.

It took almost superhuman courage and stoicism to fight a battle in which the main tactic was to stand up in non-camouflaged uniforms and let the enemy fire at you, or charge, without bulletproof vests or even functional helmets, straight into the mouths of blasting cannons. One could therefore argue that all nationalities showed the same valour at Waterloo, but Bonapartist historians naturally prefer to cite their own side's accounts of the horrors of battle.

In his book *Souvenirs d'un cadet* the young Larreguy de Civrieux remembers watching cannonballs flying towards him while under orders not to move: 'The balls came at us after ricocheting off a rise in the ground, which meant that we could make out their curved trajectory before they deci-mated our ranks. Our courage was severely put to the test, and it was despairing to wait for death with total passivity, surrounded by the dying and horribly mutilated.'*

The French were of course fired up with patriotism – in contrast to Wellington's army (or so some French commen-tators allege). On the morning of the battle, the veteran Hippolyte de Mauduit describes being a man on a mission: 'Our warlike march on this magnificent morning, in the

---

* Incidentally, the saddest testimony to all this slaughter is that the following year, the fields around Waterloo yielded a bumper grain harvest – no doubt thanks to all the well-mulched human fertiliser.

beauty of nature, had something romantic about it, and yet we were going to death with self-denial and a sort of joy, because gaiety was on all our faces.'

Even the hated French royalists grudgingly admired the spirit of Napoleon's troops. Louis Rilliet de Constant, serving at the Battle of Ligny with the Prussian army, heard the cries of 'Vive l'Empereur!' as the French attacked across open ground, bombarded by cannon fire: 'What soldiers! They were a legion of heroes or demons . . . Back from the deserts of Russia and the prison ships of England, fired up by the memories of their past victories and the shame of their recent defeats, but most of all keen to achieve glory and expunge the immense misdeed of their defection to the royalist government [in 1814, while Napoleon was on Elba].'*

To the delight of French historians, the heroism of the ordinary French soldier is even confirmed by some Brits. Sir Charles Bell, a Scottish surgeon, treated and sketched the wounded during the Belgian campaign. He produced some horrifically fascinating paintings of arm stumps, entrails spilling out of a stomach wound, bullet holes in a swollen leg, and more. Bell wrote a letter to his brother George, who sent it on to Sir Walter Scott, describing a hundred or more French casualties he had seen in a hospital: 'Though wounded, exhausted, beaten, you would still conclude with me that

---

* It might seem strange for a defector to the royal cause to be calling defection an 'immense misdeed' but this only goes to show how complex the French notion of betrayal was at this time – just as it would be again after 1945, when people were trying to explain away their actions during the Nazi Occupation.

these were men capable of marching unopposed from the west of Europe to the east of Asia. Strong, thickset, hardy veterans, brave spirits and unsubdued, as they cast their wild glance upon you – their black eyes and brown cheeks finely contrasted with the fresh sheets – you would much admire their capacity of adaptation. These fellows are brought from the field after lying many days on the ground; many dying – many in agony – many miserably racked with pain and spasms; and the next mimicks his fellow, and gives it a tune – *Aha, vous chantez bien!* How they are wounded you will see in my notes. But I must not have you to lose the present impression on me of the formidable nature of these fellows as exemplars of the breed in France.'

III

As we saw in Chapter 3, most glorious of all were the *Garde Impériale*, who are described in French accounts as though they were Leonidas' 300 Spartans holding off a million Persians. General Cambronne's men who refused to surrender are depicted as history's winners, even if they eventually got shredded into flesh fragments by point-blank cannon fire, gaining no strategic advantage in the process – unlike Leonidas, who kept the invading Persians at bay for two days while the bulk of the Greek army was able to retreat.

The *Garde Impériale* was divided into three units – the *Jeune* (Young), the *Moyenne* (Medium) and the *Vieille* (Old). *Moyenne* could also mean 'average', but mediocrity wasn't what Napoleon had in mind. The titles simply referred to the order in which the different parts of the *Garde* had been created – *Vieille* in 1804, *Moyenne* in 1806, *Jeune* in 1808.

The *Vieille Garde* were known as the *élite de l'élite*, and were treated more like Napoleon's brothers in arms than his cannon fodder. Some of the men at Waterloo had been with the Emperor throughout his career. One of the reasons he held them in reserve until the last moment was that he didn't want to lose too many of his most experienced troops in the early, wasteful stages of a battle.

To join the Old Guard, a man had to have at least ten years of army service, know how to read and write, and possess a spotless record and at least one citation for bravery. They had their own traditions, such as wearing their hair in a powdered plait that they called their *queue*, or tail (the word also means 'penis'). This was to help ward off treacherous sabre blows from behind. They also wore earrings – many of which were ripped out by corpse robbers after Waterloo. And the *Vieille Garde* always carried purses so that they could buy food and drink honourably rather than steal it.

All in all, they set themselves above the common French soldier – literally. A *Vieille Garde* had to stand at least 'cinq pieds six pouces' tall – five feet six inches (yes at that time the French still used imperial measures) – though most were taller. It is said that the men of the two battalions of Premiers Grénadiers de la Garde at Waterloo were six feet four inches tall on average. With their foot-high fur busbies, they must have looked like giants.

The *Garde Impériale*'s greatest strength was their sense of unity in defence of their Emperor. When formed up in a square they were said to be impregnable. No one except Napoleon himself and his staff was allowed to break the line and enter their square for protection. General Petit, one of the Old Guard's commanders, boasted that 'We would fire on anyone who approached, be they friend or foe, for fear of letting one in with the other. It was a necessary evil.'

In his poem 'Waterloo', Victor Hugo depicts these heroes marching gloriously to their death in their last-ditch charge, like the heroes of one of the French tragedies that Napoleon loved to watch:

Knowing that they were going to die,
They saluted their god, erect in the storm,
Their mouths crying as one 'Vive l'Empereur!',
Then, slowly, to the beat of the drums,
Smiling calmly at the English grapeshot,
The Imperial Guard stepped into the furnace.
[. . .]
They walked, cradling their weapons, head held high, grave, stoical,
Not one of them retreated. Sleep, heroic dead!

To quote a more recent French historian, Jean Thiry, writing in the mid-twentieth century about the French soldiers at Waterloo: 'The immortal page of glory that they wrote has made these defeated men the purest heroes in

French history.' And Thiry was a member of the Académie Française, so (to French minds at least) his opinion is incontestable.

IV

Even more important than this general heroism is General Cambronne's celebrated use of the word *merde* on the evening of 18 June. This, for Victor Hugo and others, was the supreme moment of the battle.

To neutral and Bonapartist commentators alike, Cambronne's defiance as his square of *Vieille Garde* stood facing a line of British cannons just 60 metres away was even more impressive than US Army General McAuliffe's famous 'nuts' in reply to a Nazi invitation to surrender at the Battle of the Bulge in 1944. McAuliffe's GIs were dug in and awaiting reinforcements. Cambronne's men were standing alone and surrounded by cannons in a cornfield.

Versions of the Cambronne legend vary. In Chapter 3, we saw Cambronne joking that he couldn't have said that the *Garde* dies rather than surrenders because he had done neither – he had in fact been wounded in the final onslaught, and taken prisoner. The consensus since then has been that Cambronne's call for heroic death was probably invented for him by a dramatist called Michel-Nicolas Balison de Rougemont.

It has also been alleged that Hugo invented the *merde* episode in his novel *Les Misérables*. But according to the nineteenth-century French historian Henry Houssaye, the use of the M-word was highly credible, because Cambronne was a battle-hardened soldier, well known for his love of swearing. Cambronne himself later admitted that he said 'some less brilliant words, with a more soldier-like energy' than his supposed 'never surrender' statement. And a sergeant at the battle told Captain Lemonnier-Delafosse that Cambronne shouted, 'Merde! I won't surrender!'

In any case, Hugo goes as far as to claim that Cambronne's defiance was more than mere heroism – with his single expletive, Hugo says, Cambronne stole overall victory for France: 'The man who won the Battle of Waterloo wasn't Napoleon in retreat; it wasn't Wellington who buckled at four o'clock, and was in despair by five, nor Blücher who didn't even fight; the man who won the Battle of Waterloo was Cambronne. Unleashing deadly lightning with such a word counts as victory.'

Hugo devotes a whole chapter of *Les Misérables* to what he calls 'this word of titanic disdain', and makes fun of the British: 'to encompass this victory in one supreme word that is impossible for them to pronounce is to lose the battlefield but win the battle. After the carnage, having laughter on your side is immense.'

In short, for Hugo, Cambronne's single syllable was more lethal than every cannonball and musket shot fired on that day.

However, one novelist's opinion doesn't explain why the story of Cambronne's legendary swearword has lived on, and even entered the French language. There were no doubt plenty of curses flying around the battlefield that day, in many different languages, but almost as soon as Cambronne's *merde* was uttered, the French showed a deep psychological need to cling on to it, and to the men it was associated with, as something deeply meaningful. This *merde* seems to have been vital to France's psyche as the nation came to terms with Waterloo and a new period of foreign occupation. And it grew in importance as the nineteenth century progressed, without – as Hugo pointed out – the vast, controlling presence of Napoleon. This was especially true after the swift, humiliating defeat in the 1870 Prussian war, when the French were desperately in need of heroes. Then, with the Prussians again marching victoriously through the Arc de Triomphe, France looked back on Napoleon and Waterloo as a period of national greatness and unity, apparently forgetting that it had all ended in bloodshed and exile.

But even before 1870, the French had begun glorifying Waterloo and saying *merde* to historical truth. *Les Misérables* was published in 1862. In 1864 and 1865, the writers Emile Erckmann and Alexandre Chatrian co-published a pair of patriotic novels, *The Conscript of 1813* and *Waterloo*, both of which were big hits.

In a similar vein, a picture painted in 1852 by Clément-Auguste Andrieux depicts a surging mass of French cavalrymen emerging from the smoke to crush a line of panicking British redcoats. It is a classic case of French cherry-picking, a picture of a successful charge that occurred at around three p.m. The scene certainly doesn't warrant the all-embracing title *La Bataille de Waterloo 18 juin 1815*.

Above: Napoleon the modern military dictator. With one 90-degree twist of the hat in 1801, he created an instantly recognisable image. His trademark black '*bicorne*' hats, worn with the points to the side, were famous throughout Europe – and still are.

However, when Napoleon had himself painted by Ingres in 1806 (left), he made a political mistake. His emperor's robes alienated him from his core supporters – and especially his fellow soldiers. Thereafter, he always reverted to the black hat and uniform in official portraits.

Napoleon was idolised by his soldiers, and was nicknamed 'the little corporal' by veterans – not because of his size but because of his youth and courage.

Right: Napoleon's favourite gesture to his men – the pinch on the ear.

Below: When Napoleon abdicated for the first time in April 1814, he gave a moving farewell speech that had his battle-hardened men in tears. The sentimental scene is re-enacted every year at the Château de Fontainebleau.

Left: His hat off, his boots dirty, Napoleon contemplates defeat in 1814. This picture was painted by Paul Delaroche in 1840, the year Napoleon's remains were returned to France. It sealed his popular status as a martyred hero.

Below: A less sympathetic British image. Napoleon, guided by the Devil and Death, has returned to power and is planning 'more horrors'. The cartoon was published by Thomas Rowlandson on 16 April 1815, almost exactly two months before Waterloo.

Above: A very French view of Waterloo, Napoleon and his soon-to-be tragic heroes.

Left: The marshals who are lambasted by Bonapartists for disobeying Napoleon's orders. From the top, the impetuous Ney, the inefficient Soult and the absentee Grouchy.

Right: The key moment of the battle for Bonapartists: General Cambronne says '*merde*' to the English. Victor Hugo claimed that this act won the day for France.

Edité par la **CHOCOLATERIE D'AIGUEBELLE**, Monastère de la Trappe (Drôme).

CAMBRONNE A WATERLOO

Above: The 'sunken lane' that broke the great French cavalry charge at Waterloo was in fact a legend created by Victor Hugo.

Top right: The victors, Blücher and Wellington, meet after Waterloo. According to Bonapartist historians it was an anticlimax as neither spoke the other's language.

Right: Napoleon sails into exile, watched by the men who were to accompany him to Saint Helena. Painted in 1880 by William Orchardson, it shows that Napoleon's legend was already established in Britain.

Waterloo – Rencontre de Wellington et Blucher devant la Belle-Alliance, se saluant mutuellement vainqueurs.

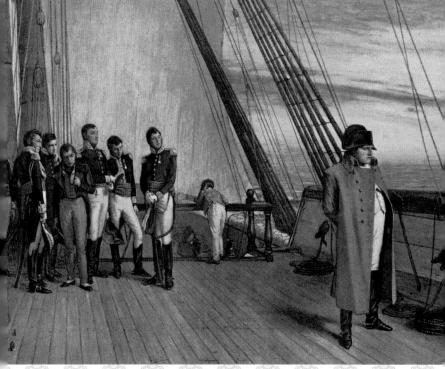

When Napoleon's remains arrived in Paris in 1840, about one million people lined the streets of Paris – in temperatures of minus ten degrees Centigrade. His golden chariot, pulled by 24 horses, and the reverential military escort quashed all notions that Napoleon Bonaparte was anything other than a victorious hero.

In 1898, Napoleon gets top billing on the posters for Buffalo Bill's Wild West show, which toured America and Europe and was seen by millions. It was the pre-cinema equivalent of achieving Hollywood superstardom.

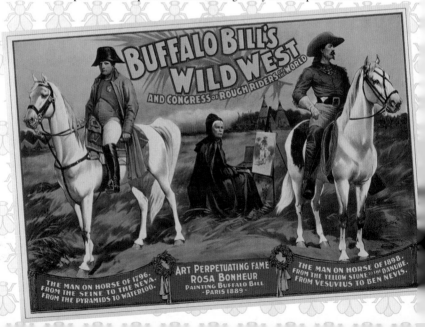

But in 1852, with Napoleon's nephew, Napoléon III, installed as emperor, France needed to be reminded that the Bonaparte family – and the country – had a glorious past.

Incidentally, Napoléon III disliked the painting because it didn't show his uncle – in his view French glory had to be inextricably linked to the Bonapartes. Today, a lot of French historians would agree with him.

This nostalgia for past glory probably explains why the French celebrate the famous 'Taxis de la Marne', the fleet of 600 Parisian taxis that ferried soldiers to the front line in September 1914 to halt the German advance towards Paris. In fact, the 4,000 or so men who went out in the taxis were mainly reservists, and didn't contribute much to the fighting, but this doesn't matter – the important thing is that the French were saying *merde* to the enemy by all means possible.

In the same way, they are keen to remember the Occupation as a time when France was almost entirely populated by a mixture of Nazi invaders and French Resistance fighters. They need to believe that, as a nation, they didn't just lay down their arms and surrender to Hitler. The Resistance hung in there, blowing up bridges, assassinating Nazi officers and generally saying *merde* to the occupiers.

This is the only way to counteract the effect of British and American jokes about French submissiveness during World War Two. There is the old one about why Napoleon planted plane trees along France's main roads – so the Germans could invade in the shade. These jibes hurt the French, as does any reference to the surrender of 1940, which is why they cling on to Napoleon's glory.

To the *merde*-sayers, it doesn't matter if France did lose the Battle of Waterloo. Dominique de Villepin argues that Cambronne and Napoleon created a French taste for glorious defeat. It is what he calls a 'new idea of Frenchness' – a feeling that France is doomed to lose but will always remain defiant. In short, *merde* to everyone and everything.

This *merde* began shaping the national character immediately after the Napoleonic Wars, when France was able to treasure its role as Europe's defeated power, and even to relish the fact that it was lagging behind in the Industrial Revolution. In 1822, the writer Chateaubriand went to England and turned his intellectual nose up at what he saw there. In the past, England had been 'covered in livestock' and generally 'charming'. Now, he said, 'its valleys are darkened by the smoke of forges and factories, its lanes turned into iron ruts, and travelling along these lanes, instead of Milton and Shakespeare, one meets mobile furnaces'. Oxford and Cambridge 'look deserted, their colleges and gothic chapels, half-abandoned, are eyesores'. England had obviously sold its soul to the gods of industry and was losing its identity just so that it could export its cheap goods all over the world. But thanks to Cambronne, the French had an answer. *Merde* to the English – we will stick to hand-making cheese, wine, fine clothes and sausages.*

Today, this *merde* attitude allows the French to claim that

* For more about the French scorn for the Industrial Revolution, see Chapter 9.

their whole culture is superior to all others. So what if Hollywood makes blockbuster superhero movies that French cinemagoers love to watch instead of homemade French dramas about adultery among the Parisian middle classes? *Merde!* The French state will keep on subsidising films that no one goes to see – at least they're French.

The same applies to language. Emerging nations prefer to speak English rather than French? *Merde* to them – it's only because, with Napoleon out of the way, the Anglos were able to colonise the world.

In terms of leaving a lasting mark on the French national psyche, Cambronne certainly won a glorious victory on 18 June 1815.

5

~

NAPOLEON FLEES . . . TO VICTORY

'Il fait le choix de la grandeur en s'abandonnant à son vain-
queur.'
'His [Napoleon's] decision to surrender to his conqueror shows
his greatness.'
– Dominique de Villepin, former French Prime Minister

'Sa chute fut gigantesque, en proportion de sa gloire.'
'His fall was gigantic, in proportion to his glory.'
– Charles de Gaulle, former President of France

I

Naturally, Napoleon does not get a universal thumbs-up
from the French for providing their country with its opportunity to play the glorious loser. His most vehement French
critic is probably Jean Jaurès, the founding father of France's
Socialist party, who in 1911 published a book with the rather

117

frightening title *The New Army: the Socialist Organization of France*, in which he twisted the knife in the old wound of Waterloo: 'Napoleon suffered a double defeat: both military and political. Politically and socially, his whole system collapsed.' Jaurès lambasted the glorification of Waterloo as 'a mortal peril for . . . the military institution and for national defence'. Logical, really – no nation wants an army that thinks it's cool to lose.

Of course Waterloo wasn't the first time Napoleon had lost on the battlefield. But in the past he had always bounced back. And in 1815, so say his fans, he could have gone on to win the war if he hadn't been prevented from doing so by his own back-stabbing compatriots.

On the morning of 19 June, Napoleon stopped at an inn, the Lion d'Or at Philippeville, south of Charleroi, Belgium, and devoured bread and butter, eggs and wine – his first meal for twenty-four hours. He was obviously still feeling bullish, because he sent a summons to Grouchy. The errant marshal still had 33,000 men under his control, and had finally got himself back into the Emperor's good books. After his *promenade militaire* of the previous day, Grouchy had tracked down a Prussian army and given them a sound beating at around eleven o'clock at night – in theory, therefore, France had won the last battle of the day. Now Napoleon wanted these victorious troops to come and rally his own demotivated army of 40,000 survivors and form a rearguard. And as Wellington later admitted, 'If he [Napoleon] had put himself at the head of that army, we were in a scrape.'

Fortified by his breakfast, Napoleon dictated a letter to

his brother Joseph: 'All is not lost. I think that when I have regrouped all my forces, I will have 150,000 men. The provincial guards and the national guards, who are fit for combat, will provide 100,000 and the regimental depots another 50,000. So I can immediately have 300,000 soldiers ready to oppose the enemy. The English march slowly, and the Prussians are afraid of peasants and won't dare advance too far. There is still time to save the situation.'

Bonapartist historians are keen to point out that when you add Wellington's view that Napoleon's 'presence on the field made the difference of 40,000 men', there was no reason why Waterloo should have been the end of the Napoleonic era, or even the end of the June campaign. Napoleon could have fought on over the following weeks, and won.

But once the effect of the Belgian eggs wore off, things obviously didn't look so bright to Napoleon, because his will began to waver. Instead of waiting for Grouchy, he fled to Paris – or rather, as his admirers would have it, he bravely rushed back to rally a defeatist parliament and save the country. The previous year, he had been betrayed by Talleyrand, who had delivered France to the royalists. Now he had to take the situation in hand, and quickly.

Napoleon knew that Joseph Fouché, the head of his Ministry of Police, was plotting his downfall, largely by manipulating the press (a job Napoleon had usually reserved for himself). Fouché was yet another of Napoleon's unwise appointments: everyone knew he was as slippery as a jar of French asparagus preserved in olive oil. For a start, he had overt royalist sympathies, and in 1814 he had negotiated a secret peace with England while Napoleon was theoretically still in power. Even so, Napoleon had made him head of the secret police on his return from exile in March 1815, probably reasoning that it was better to have Fouché as an ally than an enemy – the man was a monster. During the Revolution, Fouché had suppressed an uprising in Lyon by having more than 1,600 locals lined up and blown to pieces by cannon fire, arguing that the guillotine would have been too slow. (Even Robespierre expressed his horror at the slaughter, which was a bit like Jean-Paul Sartre accusing someone of being too intellectual.) Fouché had defended himself by saying that 'the blood of crime fertilises the soil of liberty', which was the kind of slogan that went down well during the French Revolution.

In any case, Fouché had been forgiven by Napoleon (perhaps on the grounds that he was a fellow lover of the cannon), and was now busily stabbing his employer in the back. As Napoleon sped towards Paris, Fouché circulated a rumour that he was returning to impose a military dictatorship. The secret policeman also assured parliament that if Napoleon was forced to abdicate, the allies would not insist on another restoration of the monarchy – there would (Fouché lied) be another revolution, opening the way for parliament to grab absolute power.

When Napoleon arrived back in Paris on 21 June, Fouché gleefully told everyone that the fallen Emperor was a changed man: 'unrecognisable . . . he hopes, he despairs, he wants, he doesn't want. He's lost his head.' The last sentence might have been a clever piece of subliminal suggestion, hinting that Napoleon should suffer the same fate as Louis XVI.

In fact, on reaching the city before dawn, Napoleon made two perfectly reasonable requests: he wanted his ministers and a bath. Not to enjoy a communal soak, but so that he could put in an immediate demand for 'a temporary dictatorship'. Fouché, it seemed, was right. And Napoleon's behaviour in the bathtub seemed to confirm Fouché's other allegation – that he had lost his head – because during the meeting the agitated Emperor waved his arms about, splashing all those present with his dirty bathwater. He tried to explain that he needed complete power 'in the interests of the nation. I could seize it, but it would be more useful and more national if it was conferred by parliament.' He wanted to relocate the government 200 kilometres south-west in Tours, prepare Paris for a siege, and begin conscripting a new army.

While the ministers dried off and presented this request to the MPs, Napoleon confided in his old friend and Minister of Foreign Affairs, Louis de Caulaincourt. It is clear that in his own head he had begun rewriting history already. 'The battle was won,' he told Caulaincourt, 'the army had been prodigious, the enemy was beaten on all fronts. Only the English centre held. Then at the end of the day, the army was seized by a terrible panic. It's inexplicable!'

The MPs, though, didn't want a repeat of recent events. They voted to divest Napoleon of all his powers, and declared that if he tried to dissolve parliament and impose military rule, he would be denounced as a traitor. For which, of course, the penalty was the guillotine or the firing squad.

Napoleon's brother Lucien went to try and talk the MPs round, accusing them of having a short memory, but the Marquis de La Fayette, hero of both the French and American Revolutions, crushed him with an impassioned speech: 'Have you forgotten that we followed him [Napoleon] through the sands of Africa and the deserts of Russia, and that the scattered bones of our children and our brothers bear witness to our fidelity? We have done enough for him. Now our duty is to save the nation.' Even so, in an admirable spirit of fair play, La Fayette offered to use his old contacts to ensure Napoleon a safe passage to America.

By now there were increasing calls for Napoleon to be handed over to the allies. The Prussians, and some of his French enemies, wanted him out of the picture permanently.

II

For once, Wellington gains brownie points with French Bonapartists, because he spoke out against executing his old enemy. In reply to a Prussian demand 'that Bonaparte be delivered over to us, with a view to execution . . . Thus the blood of our soldiers killed and mutilated on the 16th and 18th will be avenged', Wellington wrote sternly that 'Such an act would hand down our names to history stained by a crime, and posterity would say of us that we did not deserve to be the conquerors of Napoleon . . . Such a deed is quite useless and can have no object.' Wellington also wrote to his political masters, telling them that 'if the sovereigns [of the allied nations] wish him put to death they should appoint an executioner, which should not be me'.

This infuriated Blücher's chief of staff, General Gneisenau, who accused the British of feeling grateful to Napoleon for indirectly increasing their 'greatness, prosperity and wealth'. But Wellington was a soldier through and through, with a grudging respect for the great French general that Napoleon had been.

Betrayed by his own parliament and afraid of falling into Prussian hands, on the afternoon of 29 June Napoleon decided to flee towards the port of Rochefort on the British-held south-west coast, hoping for a hospitable welcome. He put on a suit of civilian clothes, climbed into a yellow carriage (an unfortunate symbolic choice of colour, one might think), and gave up the fight.

He also wrote a letter to the Prince of Wales, the Regent of England during his father George III's mental illness, begging for asylum: 'I come, like Themistocles, to ask the hospitality of the British people. I put myself under the protection of its laws, which I claim from your Royal Highness, the most powerful, the most unflinching and most generous of my enemies. I thus offer him the greatest page in his history.'

It is a strange mixture of grovelling sycophancy and self-aggrandisement. Themistocles was an Athenian who in about 470 BC took refuge with the King of the Persians, whom he had previously beaten in battle. He was received as a hero and given command of Persia's captured Greek cities in Asia Minor. Perhaps Napoleon hoped to be taken on by the Brits as the colonial governor of, say, India or Canada.

In any case, here he was, without his famous uniform, terrified of being captured by the Prussians, and begging for mercy from his former arch enemies, *les Anglais*. It was the ultimate humiliation, surely?

Well no, because according to his French fans, he was about to turn his escape into yet another victory . . .

III

Back in London, the British press was indulging in a frenzy of triumphalism over Waterloo. Public enemy number one had been beaten into submission, and the war was over. On 22 June, *The Times* declared jingoistically – and prematurely – that 'Buonaparte's reputation has been wrecked' (note the deliberate use of the old Corsican spelling of Napoleon's name that he had tried to disown). In the same edition, the paper called him a 'Rebel Chief', as if he were a brigand rather than a head of state, and boasted that among the spoils of war were 'a large part of BUONAPARTE'S BAGGAGE' (their capitals), implying perhaps that the war correspondent would soon be revealing details about the Emperor's captured underwear.

On that same day, by coincidence, *The Times* printed a classified advertisement placed by 'a French Gentleman' who was 'desirous to BOARD and LODGE in a genteel family whose society would enable him to improve in the English language'. Answers were to be sent to a mysterious 'XY, c/o Carraway's Coffee House'. Was this Napoleon, planning his exile?

Almost certainly not, because even a week after the advert was placed, Napoleon still hadn't made up his mind what to do. As late as the morning of 29 June, he still thought he could fight on. He had formally abdicated, but just before he got into his yellow carriage to Rochefort, a group of soldiers came and begged him to lead them into battle. They told him that the Prussian avant-garde had advanced too far, that it had moved beyond Paris and was exposed. Napoleon studied charts of the Prussian positions and agreed that he could go and beat them. He put on his uniform, and sent a request to parliament for permission to fight – as a mere general, if not as Emperor. Furious, Fouché dismissed the idea: 'Est-ce qu'il se moque de nous?' Which could be translated as 'Is he taking the pee?'

Napoleon was deadly serious, though, and was proved right when, on 1 July, one of his most faithful generals, Rémy Exelmans, attacked and defeated the Prussians at Rocquencourt, 20 kilometres south-west of Paris. Exelmans had been frustrated at Waterloo – he was one of the generals who spent the day pleading with Grouchy to march towards the sound of Napoleon's cannons, and (it is said) even considered blowing Grouchy's brains out. Now, with about 5,000 men, Exelmans ambushed a force of a thousand or so Prussian cavalry, killing or capturing 500 of them.

Rocquencourt was in effect the last battle of the Napoleonic Wars – a general armistice was signed on 3 July – which allows the French a certain amount of triumphalism of their own. They might have been defeated at Waterloo and lost the war on points, but who won the final round of this European all-comers championship fight? France.*

IV

Even the armistice did not dampen Napoleon's desire to retake charge of his remaining troops. On 7 July, now in Rochefort on the south-west coast, he sent another message to Paris, asking parliament whether they might consider letting him 'sauver la patrie' ('save the nation'). His plan, according to one of his aides, General Charles de Montholon, was to 'march on Paris at the head of twenty to twenty-five thousand soldiers, with a people's escort of a hundred thousand fanatical peasants'.

The reply was predictable but ominous. Napoleon was told by his own government to board a French ship and await further orders. He must have known that once in the hands of pro-royalist forces, the danger was that he would be used as a hostage during negotiations with the allies, and who knew where that would leave him? Up against a wall in Paris, probably, facing a line of Blücher's muskets.

In an uncharacteristic turmoil of indecision, Napoleon was still vacillating between taking exile in Britain or, more adventurously, in America. At one point he invited a seventy-year-old politician and mathematician, Gaspard Monge, to embark on a voyage of scientific discovery as his travelling

---

* See my book *1000 Years of Annoying the French* to find out how France used this victory at Rocquencourt to win yet another battle over the Anglo-Saxon enemy almost 150 years later.

companion. 'Without an army or an empire, I see nothing but the sciences to occupy my soul,' Napoleon wrote to Monge. 'I want to start a new career, to leave a body of work, of discoveries worthy of my name.' Having given France a set of laws to obey, Napoleon seems to have wanted to do the same thing for the whole physical universe. He offered Monge the honour of accompanying him 'from Canada to Cape Horn, and during this immense voyage, we will study all the great phenomena of the globe's physics'. Monge was all for the idea, and the two men even drew up a shortlist of scientific instruments that they would need; but then Napoleon abruptly backed out, deciding that Monge was too old for such transatlantic exertions.

Finally, after a month during which his mind had been clinging to a stampeding charger that galloped between optimism and resignation, Napoleon now came to a decision. He gave himself up to the British. Some Bonapartists see turning to the hereditary enemy as a sign of weakness, of naivety even – how could he possibly trust *Perfide Albion*? But Dominique de Villepin interprets it as an honourable decision, and a more intellectually respectable one: Napoleon could have run away to America, but 'there was a certain nobility about turning to this hereditary enemy', the 'model of an aristocratic monarchy that this history-lover, imbued with tradition, probably admired more than the young American democracy'. (As we have seen, democracy wasn't exactly Napoleon's thing.)

At about six a.m. on 15 July, Napoleon duly left the small offshore island île d'Aix, where he had been hiding, and boarded the British warship HMS *Bellerophon* that was blockading the port of Rochefort. It has been said that the *Bellerophon* was effectively preventing Napoleon from fleeing to America, but Bonapartist historians sneer at this suggestion. Hadn't Napoleon already evaded a joint Franco-British blockade around Elba? Did they really think he couldn't have disguised himself as a fisherman and joined a friendly ship offshore? No, the decision to surrender to the British was a conscious choice, albeit a symbolically charged one, as *Bellerophon* had fought at Trafalgar, the sea battle that had scuppered Napoleon's plans to invade England in 1805.

When he boarded the British ship, in full military regalia, Napoleon announced (in French, of course), 'I come aboard your ship to place myself under the protection of your prince and your laws.' To Bonapartists, this was a kind of chivalrous surrender that ought to have bound the British to act honourably, and it makes their later actions all the more treacherous.

At first, Napoleon's reception seemed to be cordial. There is a wonderful description of his time on the *Bellerophon* written by an officer who saw it all first-hand. It is quoted with relish by Bonapartist historians. Writing in 1838, Midshipman George Home recalled the Emperor's arrival on the ship: 'And now came the little great man himself, wrapped up in his grey great coat, buttoned to the chin, three-cocked hat, and Hussar boots, without any sword I suppose as emblematical of his changed condition.'

The young Englishman was shocked to note his own captain's somewhat aloof behaviour towards his esteemed French visitor: 'Maitland received him with every mark of respect, as far as look and deportment could indicate; but

he was not received with the respect due to a crowned head
. . . The captain, on Napoleon's addressing him, only moved
his hat, as to a general officer, and remained covered while
the Emperor spoke to him.'

The effect on the other sailors, on the other hand, was
very different. A superstar had arrived. If it had happened
in the twenty-first century, the men would all have been
taking selfies. Midshipman Home, who seems to have fallen
in love with Napoleon at first sight, remembered that 'As
he passed through the officers assembled on the quarter-
deck, he repeatedly bowed slightly to us and smiled. What
an ineffable beauty there was in that smile. His teeth were
finely set, and as white as ivory, and his mouth had a charm
about it that I have never seen in any other human countenance. I marked his fine robust figure as he followed
Captain Maitland into the cabin.'

Napoleon appears to have bonded instantly with these
fighting men, and asked to tour the ship. Now that he was
no longer a military threat, his wish was granted, and he
did the rounds, complimenting the British sailors on the
fine state of their vessel, and winning over even the hard-
hearted captain. Napoleon paused in front of one of George
Home's fellow midshipmen: 'A young middy who, boylike,
had got before the Emperor and was gazing up in his face,
he honoured with a tap on the head and a pinch of the ear,
and, smiling, put him aside, which the youngster declared
was the highest honour he had ever received in his life viz.
to have his ears pinched by the great Napoleon!'

After this, all British sailors, including some admirals

who came to take a look at their star guest, doffed their hats to Napoleon, much to Midshipman Home's satisfaction: 'When Admiral Hotham and the officers of the *Bellerophon* uncovered in the presence of Napoleon, they treated him with the respect due to the man himself, to his innate greatness, which did not lie in the crown of France . . . but the actual superiority of the man to the rest of his species.'

The Bonaparte legend was being born, and Napoleon must have felt that his retirement wasn't going to be so bad after all. He inspected the contingent of marines on board, and asked them to perform some drill. Flatteringly, he even risked a joke, exclaiming, 'What I could do with 200,000 men like these!' Diplomatically ignoring the obvious answer, which was 'kill as many Englishmen as possible and then invade Britain', Midshipman Home heartily approved of the remark: 'And so you well might say, my most redoubtable Emperor, for, give you two hundred thousand such fine fellows as these, and land you once more at Rochefort, and I shall be sworn for it that in three short weeks you have Wellington and the Holy Allies flying before you in every direction, and in ten days more you have the imperial headquarters at Schonbrunn [in Vienna].'

In short, thanks to his charisma and his sincere fascination for all things military, Napoleon had won over the British crew's hearts. He had also earned their protection. There would be no French or Prussian delegations coming on board to take Napoleon into custody now. Neither would any other British vessel get the honour of transporting the deposed *Empereur* to Britain. The crew of the *Bellerophon* swore that they would resist by force any attempt to take Napoleon off their ship.

However, as Bonapartist historians are all too happy to point out, this sudden outburst of British brotherly love for Napoleon was too good to be true. The *Anglais* were about to betray him . . .

V

There is a famous painting of *Napoleon on Board the Bellerophon* by the Scottish portraitist William Quiller Orchardson. It was first exhibited in 1880, and was such a success with Londoners at that year's Royal Academy summer exhibition that it inspired Orchardson to follow up with a series of French-themed pictures, including one of the writer Voltaire getting beaten up by the servants of an aristocrat whom he had unwisely insulted.

Orchardson depicts Napoleon, in trademark hat and greatcoat, gazing gloomily out to sea. His expression is an archetypal French pout. He is sullenly turning his back on a small group of his aides, their hats held respectfully by their sides, who are observing him with a combination of curiosity, concern, sadness and resignation. They seem to be wondering whether he will jump overboard, start weeping, or suddenly order them to seize control of the ship and invade England.

It's an atmospheric painting, and is meant to show the moment on 31 July when Napoleon learned that, contrary to his expectation, he would not be settling in England and writing his memoirs between visits from admiring *Anglaises* – he was being sent into exile on Saint Helena, a British rock in the middle of the South Atlantic vividly described by one of Napoleon's entourage, General Bertrand, as 'an island shat by the devil'.

There had been rumours about Saint Helena in the British press, and Napoleon had definitely heard them, but confirmation of the news must have come as a hammer blow. Until that moment, the journey from Rochefort back to England had been more like a pleasure cruise. Midshipman Home described the ship's arrival in Torbay. Some of the officers were given permission to go ashore and 'I was taken prisoner by some twenty young ladies, marched off to a fine house in the little town, regaled with tea and clouted [*sic*] cream, and bored with five thousand questions about Napoleon, the ridiculousness of which I have often laughed at since: What was he like? Was he really a man? Were his hands and clothes all over blood when he came on board? Was it true that he had killed three horses in riding from Waterloo to the *Bellerophon*? Were we not all frightened of him? Was his voice like thunder?'

Shore leave spent fighting off Napoleon's groupies (and probably surrendering to at least one) – it was a young sailor's dream. At Plymouth two days later, Home wrote that things got even more hysterical, as about 1,000 boats swarmed around the *Bellerophon*, hoping to get closer to the world-famous Frenchman: 'He must have conceived that he was as much admired by the English as by his own beloved French. The Sound was literally covered with boats; the weather was delightful; the ladies looked as gay as butterflies; bands of music in several of the boats played favourite French airs, to attract, if possible, the Emperor's attention, that they might get a sight of him, which, when effected, they went off, blessing themselves that they had been so fortunate . . . He showed no disinclination to gratify the eager spectators, by frequently appearing at the gangway, examining the crowd with his pocket-glass; and frequently, as a pretty face gazed at him with bewitching curiosity, he showed his fine white teeth, lifted the little three-cocked hat nearly off his broad and commanding forehead, for he never wholly uncovered, bowed, and smiled with evident satisfaction.'

Then the order arrived from London, condemning Napoleon to distant exile, and everything changed. No longer was he 'Monsieur the Emperor'. He was a dangerous prisoner of war. Customs men came aboard and even seized a few dozen bottles of French wine that Napoleon had given to the captain's wife, Mrs Maitland.

Midshipman Home was furious about the mistreatment: 'I never think of the proceedings which I then witnessed without feeling my blood boil up with indignation, and my face blush crimson for my degraded country.'

Understandably, Napoleon suddenly felt less sociable, and disappeared below deck. When he was transferred to the HMS *Northumberland* – supposedly a newer, more reliable ship than the *Bellerophon** – for transport to Saint Helena,

---

* After this mission, HMS *Bellerophon* was converted into a prison ship, and in case its future occupants misinterpreted their status, as Napoleon had done, it was renamed the *Captivity*.

the deposed Emperor was a changed man: 'His clothes were ill put on, his beard unshaved, and his countenance pale and haggard. There was a want of firmness in his gait, his brow was overcast, and his whole visage bespoke the deepest melancholy; and it needed but a glance to convince the most careless observer that Napoleon considered himself a doomed man . . . The ship's deck looked like a place of execution, and we only wanted the headsman, his block, and his axe to complete the scene.'

Midshipman Home, a lifelong Napoleon fan, concludes his account of the episode with a prescient accolade that is a favourite among Bonapartists: 'The more the character of Napoleon gains its true place in the page of history, the more dastardly will appear our conduct.' As we will see in Chapter 8, the young officer's prediction was completely accurate.

VI

However, it would be a mistake to think that Napoleon let himself go to Saint Helena without a fight. He was furious, and dictated a statement of protest: 'I came aboard *Bellerophon* of my own free will. I am not a prisoner, I am a guest of England . . . I appeal to History, which will say that an enemy who waged war on the English people for twenty years came freely, in his hour of misfortune, to seek asylum under its laws. What more striking proof of his esteem and trust could he give?'

This wasn't a letter to the Prince Regent or the British government. It was simply a statement of his opinion, an historical record. Napoleon was already thinking of himself as a sort of living monument. And he was right to do so. History has judged the British for this 'betrayal' – or a certain strain of French historians has done, anyway. The modern Bonapartist writer Jean-Claude Damamme expresses 'a profound distaste for England, which brought dishonour upon itself that nothing will ever wash away'.

Again, the Bonapartists manage to extract a victory from this new British slap in the face. If the English felt obliged to send Napoleon to the other end of the earth, it was because they were terrified of him, *n'est-ce pas*?

British sources prove it: Lady Charlotte Fitzgerald, the wife of a British MP, for example, saw Napoleon transferred from the *Bellerophon* to the *Northumberland*, and wrote that 'Others may suppose his career finished but I am sure he does not – he appears most to resemble a bust of marble or bronze as cold and as fixed. He seems quite inaccessible to human tenderness or human distress.' Lady Charlotte recalled that she 'came away with my heart Considerably Steeled against him, & with many fears lest the Lion again escape from his Cage'. (Though she also noted that 'he is wonderful!'.)

Another Englishwoman described the crowds who came to see Napoleon in Plymouth, and concluded, 'His person is so prepossessing that it is dangerous to the loyalty of the people.'

Wellington himself seems to have agreed with this point of view. According to his friend and confidante Lady Frances Shelley, the Iron Duke was relieved that the British government had refused to let Napoleon land in England. 'It was only by coercion . . . that they prevented George the Fourth from receiving Bonaparte,' Wellington reportedly said. 'There can be little doubt that if Bonaparte had got to London, the Whig Opposition were ready to use him as their trump card, to overturn the Government!'

Et voilà, Napoleon's admirers can cheer: Wellington himself was still scared, even after Waterloo. Napoleon's charisma was so powerful that, even unarmed and almost unaccompanied, he could not be permitted to set foot on English soil. His very presence would have undermined the British government and caused rebellion, both at home and in France. Who knows, Napoleon might even have succeeded in convincing a new Whig government to lend him British soldiers (including Wellington) so that he could recapture his throne.

That might be idle Bonapartist fantasy (though no fantasy seems too great when it comes to Napoleon's most fervent admirers), but one thing is for certain: over the 200 years since Napoleon set off for Saint Helena, his stature has never stopped growing. It has been, as Victor Hugo said, a case of 'losing the field but keeping control of history'.

Because no matter who ended up claiming control of a few hectares of blood-soaked Belgian farmland, Napoleon's many fans will claim – with some justification – that only one man has come to stand triumphant over the battlefield of history, overshadowing everyone else who was involved in the fighting on 18 June 1815.

WARM FUZZY GLOW – TO GO

Every item you buy or donate helps lift lives worldwide. Just £6 raised could train a health volunteer, helping communities in Bangladesh prepare for disaster.

www.oxfam.org.uk

LIFT
LIVES
FOR
GOOD |  OXFAM

TAKE HOME SOME NECTAR POINTS

Donate your unwanted items to Oxfam and you can collect Nectar points when they're sold.
Find out more at:

PART TWO

6

ABSENCE MAKES THE (FRENCH) HEART GROW FONDER

'Napoléon a accru le patrimoine d'héroïsme de la France.'
'Napoleon increased France's national stock of heroism.'
     – from the review of a book about Waterloo
      in the magazine *Lectures pour Tous* (1898)

'Une défaite est l'expiation d'une gloire passée et souvent le garant d'une victoire pour l'avenir.'
'A defeat is an atonement for past glory, and often the guarantee of future victory.'
    – Ernest Renan, nineteenth-century French philosopher

I

When Napoleon arrived on Saint Helena on 15 October 1815, he was justifiably depressed. Elba had been within sight of mainland Italy, almost within swimming distance of his native Corsica, and peopled by adoring natives and hundreds of faithful *Gardes*. Saint Helena was 2,000 miles from the nearest continent, further away from France than Napoleon had ever been. Even the snowy wastes of Russia were on the doorstep compared to this lonely rock.

And this time Napoleon was no island sovereign, with a friendly governor to keep a casual eye on him. He was a prisoner watched over by 125 British guards, and hemmed in by a ring of hostile British ships with orders to fire on any unauthorised vessel approaching the island. Instead of the army that had accompanied Napoleon to Elba, he was attended by only two dozen people – three generals and their families, a secretary, and a skeleton staff of servants. Not only that, the coffee, bread and wine were disgusting, and random Englishmen could enter his room at any time and speak to him without asking permission. A firing squad, the deposed Emperor complained, 'would have been a blessing by comparison'.

To cap it all, he was given a mean-spirited jailer who, it quickly became clear, had been entrusted with the job of making Napoleon's existence a living hell.

A man of the same age as Napoleon (he was born two weeks before his famous prisoner), Sir Hudson Lowe was an old soldier whose path had very nearly crossed that of his French captive several times during the Napoleonic Wars. Lowe had been sent to Toulon just before it was liberated by the young Napoleon in 1793. He had then been posted on the island of Corsica (when it was briefly under British control) and even billeted at the Buonaparte family home. Later on, he had commanded a force of pro-British Corsican exiles in the Mediterranean, a fact that irritated Napoleon considerably – he called them 'vagabond Corsican deserters'. And after serving during the 1814 campaign to oust Napoleon from power, Lowe had been chosen to take the glad tidings of his abdication to London. In French eyes, Lowe was therefore just about the most troublesome anti-Bonaparte campaigner the British government could have chosen.

Not only that, Lowe was notoriously small-minded. Aleksandr Balmain, the Russian representative on Saint Helena, said of Lowe that 'he is awkward, and impossibly unreasonable. He kills those around him with pin pricks. He has a weak, confused mind that takes fright at the slightest thing.' The complete opposite, in other words, of a courageous French general with visions of world domination.

Lowe took over the job of guarding Napoleon in April 1816, and immediately proved that he had none of Wellington's magnanimity towards his former adversary. He made sure that Napoleon's isolation in the wind-battered Longwood House, an hour's ride from the capital Jamestown, was almost complete.

Lowe was infuriatingly petty in a way that is usually the domain of French bureaucrats. He once refused to let Napoleon have a new pair of shoes until the old pair had been handed over. He also forbade the British garrison from addressing Napoleon as anything grander than 'General'. This incensed Napoleon, who declared that he wanted to change his name to Baron Duroc ('Baron of the Rock'). A neat play on words, but Lowe took it seriously and expressly forbade it.*

This wasn't the only mischief that Lowe inspired in his captive. When he ordered guards to spy openly on Napoleon, insisting that the prisoner be sighted at least once a day, Napoleon took to hiding indoors to frustrate his captors. Once, when he heard that Lowe was on his way to visit, Napoleon leapt into the bath so as to be unavailable – and later informed Lowe that he had done so. It was open rebellion.

Lowe insulted Napoleon by ordering that Saint Helena's French contingent should cover some of the expenses of their exile, though he changed his mind when Napoleon put up some of his personal silver for sale, and the demand from the outside world was so enormous that Lowe feared it would create an undesirable market in Napoleonic souvenirs.

In short, the English governor was so disrespectful to the *Empereur* that Bonapartist historians despise him even more than Blücher. There is a book called *Hudson Lowe face au jugement des Anglais* (that is, 'condemned by the English'), published in 2001, that gleefully lists Lowe's misfortunes after his time on Saint Helena. It claims that Lowe's name was dragged through the mud in 1827 by Sir Walter Scott

---

* In fact, Napoleon had thought of calling himself Duroc well before it became an appropriate pun, and used the pseudonym for his escape from Paris to Rochefort at the end of June 1815. It was the name of one of his most faithful generals, Michel Duroc, who had been with him since the siege of Toulon in 1793, who fought at the battles of Austerlitz and Wagram, and who was killed in Germany in 1813.

in his biography of Napoleon (see Chapter 7), though in fact Scott mostly defends Lowe's patience in the face of his prisoner's provocations. Scott does criticise Lowe for occasionally being over-zealous in interpreting his government's instructions, and for telling Napoleon to reduce the costs of his captivity; but after detailing every quibble and argument between prisoner and jailer, he concludes that 'reason and temper on either side would have led to a very different proceeding on both'. No matter, though – Scott's detailed examination of the charges against Lowe counts, in Bonapartist eyes, as condemnation. The *jugement des Anglais*, we are told, was a guilty verdict. After being sent into exile himself as governor of Ceylon, Lowe decided to return to Britain to defend himself, lost his job, and died in poverty. A fitting end – so the Bonapartists tell us – to Napoleon's tormentor.

According to Napoleon's admirers, his only consolation during his exile – apart from the sexual favours he obtained from the wives of his entourage – was that it gave him the chance to sit down and rewrite the story of his reign. This battle for possession of the high ground in history would be his last, and ultimately most successful, campaign.

II

Not that Napoleon rewrote events himself – his every thought was dictated to one of his most ardent fans on Saint Helena, his chamberlain and companion, Emmanuel de Las Cases.

Las Cases had accompanied Napoleon from Paris to Rochefort, and was the man who first contacted Captain Maitland of the *Bellerophon* with a view to a surrender. It has been alleged that Las Cases was too naive in his dealings with Maitland, and allowed Napoleon to fall into British hands when he would have done better to advise his employer to flee to America.

It has also been suggested that Las Cases made sure he left Saint Helena as soon as he had recorded enough material for a book. He was expelled by Hudson Lowe in 1816 – purportedly for trying to smuggle out a letter complaining about the Emperor's mistreatment – and took with him 925 pages of Napoleonic reminiscences.

Despite allegations about Las Cases' loyalty to Napoleon, when his book, *Le Mémorial de Sainte-Hélène*, was published in eight volumes in 1823, it became a bible for Bonapartists, and laid the foundations for the image of Napoleon as a combination of martyr and historical monument. Part diary, part history book, the 'memoirs' were much embellished by Las Cases, and interspersed with the author's own admiring comments, but most of all they represented a huge canvas upon which Napoleon was allowed to paint the heroic tableau of his life.

All soldiers' reminiscences are wise after the event, but in Las Cases' volumes, a worldwide audience, already fascinated by the myth of the fallen French war hero, was given a veritable feast of Napoleonic hindsight. His misunderstood desire for a Europe-wide democracy, his unacknowledged campaign for world peace, the unfairness of the weather conditions on the night of 17–18 June 1815, and of course his genius on various battlefields – Napoleon's whole career is there, in chapter after chapter of ramblings that jump from one subject to the next, from religion to rat control, from accounting to freedom of speech, and the 'folly' of equality for women.*

In the book, Napoleon explains, for example, why he was known as the *petit caporal*. It was a nickname given to him by the 'old moustaches' when he took command of the *Armée d'Italie* (that is, the army that was to invade Italy, not the Italian army) at the tender age of twenty-five. After his first victory at Lodi in northern Italy in 1796, the old soldiers showed their approval by 'promoting' him from private to corporal. Nothing to do with his diminutive size, *bien sûr*.

He denies having seized power in 1799 with a *coup d'état*: 'I didn't usurp the crown. I picked it up from the gutter. The people put it on my head.'

He claims that his only true goal as ruler of France was 'the reign of reason' – that is, to educate the people. 'What a younger generation I will leave! They are my creation. Their achievements will be my revenge.'

He recalls his great battles, of course, dishing out praise and condemnation to the officers who served him well or otherwise, and marvelling at his own judgement on the battlefield. 'Success in war,' he opines, 'hangs so much on insight and seizing the moment' – which he did, over and over again.

---

* In a peach of a sentence, Napoleon declares that a woman 'is the property of a man as a fruit tree is the property of a gardener'.

He also predicts that his future detractors will be wasting their time, or 'biting into granite' as he puts it: 'My memory consists of facts,* and mere words will not be able to destroy them.'

In this, of course, Napoleon was absolutely right, and his own war of words, the *Mémorial de Sainte-Hélène*, has since proved to be a resounding victory in allowing Bonapartists to disregard Waterloo as a minor blot on the otherwise spotless record of a national hero.

III

Back in France, it was a simple matter to turn absence into nostalgia in the years after Waterloo, because the man supposedly ruling in Napoleon's place was such an obvious disaster. Louis XVIII was totally subservient to the British and their allies. Céleste de Chateaubriand, the wife of the writer of the same name, summed up the feeling of many French people about the King in one simple sentence: 'Bonaparte came back at the head of 400 Frenchmen; Louis XVIII returned behind 400,000 foreigners.'

The corpulent monarch knew which side his bread was buttered on (both – and it was buttery brioche), and always put the allies', and his own, interests above those of France.

He didn't even gain any vicarious glory from being on the winning side at Waterloo. Louis and his 'army' of only 1,500 men had simply sat around in Ghent, fattening themselves

* Napoleon used the word *faits*, which also means 'actions'.

146

while the real soldiers were battling it out. Napoleonic veterans poured scorn on them in their memoirs. A French officer called Rilliet de Constant alleged that the battle cry of Louis XVIII's army had been 'We demand to die for our good king, and, while awaiting this beautiful moment, we demand decent lodgings and food from the Lion d'Or [Ghent's best inn]'. There, Louis was rumoured to gulp down a hundred oysters in one sitting, and gained the nickname *le roi restaurateur* (a play on 'restoration' and 'restaurant'). The townspeople would go and stare through the windows at him, and christened him 'Louis de Zweet' – a Flemish pun. When spoken, it sounds like 'Louis dix-huit' (Louis XVIII), but literally translated, it means 'Louis who Sweats' – a cruelly witty description of the gluttonous monarch.

As soon as Louis was re-established on the throne, he sent Catholic missionaries around France, 'cleansing' sensitive regions of their fanaticism for Napoleon, as though Bonapartism were a religion (which, in some ways, it was – and still is). There was also a brief 'Terreur Blanche' (white being the royal colour) in 1815, during which royalists massacred some 500 known Bonapartists in the south of France. This of course only redoubled hatred of Louis XVIII's regime, and made Napoleon appear more martyr-like before he was even dead. Faithful followers prayed for his return.

There were constant rumours that Napoleon was on his way back, either physically or in spirit. In Aube – the region where Napoleon had mounted his heroic resistance to the Prussian invasion of 1814 – a chicken was confiscated by the local gendarmes after laying an egg on which it was possible to make out an image of *l'Empereur*.

Similarly, when a street trader was arrested in Paris in 1818 for selling statues of Napoleon, he confessed (or boasted) that he had already offloaded 4,000 idols of the exiled hero.

On the other hand, in 1816, the people of Carcassonne, in the (pro-British) south-west of France, were so afraid that he would return that they burned alive a poor eagle that probably had no idea it was a Napoleonic emblem.

In short, Napoleon was still well and truly present in French minds when, in 1821, the national obsession with him was suddenly cranked up to fever pitch.

IV

A recurrent theme running throughout Las Cases' book is the outrageous disrespect shown by the British – and especially Hudson Lowe – once they had delivered the fallen Emperor (Las Cases always refers to Napoleon as 'l'Empereur') safely into exile. And this general climate of British abuse quickly provoked Bonapartists into seeing darker forces at play when their hero fell ill.

Napoleon had often suffered from stomach pains, and after a six-week spell in bed that Lowe initially suspected was play-acting (he suggested that someone should burst into Napoleon's bedroom and shock him into getting up), he died, on Saturday, 5 May 1821, at the premature age of fifty-one. His last words were probably the very apt 'tête d'armée' ('head of an army'), though we can't be sure because various patriotic and romantic sources also have him whispering sweet nothings about France and Josephine.

Napoleon once said of Lowe that 'he has crime engraved on his face', and there have long been rumours that the governor murdered his captive. Although Napoleon's father had died of stomach cancer, and it seems almost certain that Napoleon succumbed to this genetic disposition and a succession of gastric ulcers, it has often been alleged that he was poisoned with arsenic. After his death, the toxin was discovered both in samples of Napoleon's hair and in the wallpaper at Longwood. Proof, according to many Bonapartists, of foul play.

But at the time, arsenic was used as a treatment for baldness, and Napoleon often used to wash his receding locks with this toxic shampoo. Not only that, arsenic was a common component in dyes, and it would have been unwise to lick any British wallpaper of the early nineteenth century – if that is what Napoleon was driven to do by the frustration of captivity.

Nonetheless, rumours of assassination by the representative of *Perfide Albion* only served to heighten Napoleon's almost Christ-like image of martyrdom. Alongside Victor Hugo's suggestion that God decided the outcome of Waterloo, Napoleon's memoirs read like one long cry of 'why have you forsaken me?'

The Christ analogy is not an idle one. Before Napoleon died, there was already a version of the Lord's Prayer in his name, which reads something like a call for resurrection rather than a return from exile:

Notre Empereur qui êtes à Sainte-Hélène
Que votre nom soit respecté
Que votre règne revienne
Que votre volonté soit faite
Contre tous les ultras qui nous ôtent nos pensions
Débarrassez-nous des maudits Bourbons
Ainsi soit-il.*

V

The loud grumblings in France about the possibility that the British had poisoned the exiled Emperor were in no way quashed when the *Anglais* ignored Napoleon's dying wish that 'my ashes should rest by the Seine, among the French people whom I have loved so much', and dropped him into a tiny grave on Saint Helena, some 5,000 kilometres from his favourite river.

Not that Napoleon would have objected too much to his grave site on the island – it was his second choice after the Seine, in a lush valley where his servants would go and collect fresh water. And the Emperor's body was very well looked after. It was sealed inside three coffins so as to postpone putrefaction (maybe eternally, so that he could rise again?) – an outer lead casing, a walnut casket and an inner iron lining.

* Translated, this borders on the comic: 'Our Emperor who art in Saint Helena / Respected be thy name / Thy reign return / Thy will be done / Against the extremists who take away our pensions / Rid us of the accursed Bourbons / Amen.'

But this was not good enough for France, and there was always a movement within the country campaigning for their hero's homecoming. It was of course politically impossible to repatriate Napoleon's remains while the considerable bulk of Louis XVIII – or Cochon XVIII ('Pig the eighteenth') as Bonapartists had now renamed him – was occupying the throne.

Louis died in 1824, literally rotting away with gout and gangrene, to be replaced by his brother Charles X, who proved to the French that this foreign-imposed monarchy really was a bad idea by reintroducing press censorship and dissolving parliament. The MPs revolted, and Charles adopted the Bourbon family's usual tactic of fleeing into exile, updating traditions only slightly by running away to Scotland instead of England.

In 1830, France was briefly embroiled in another Napoleonic war, as the Emperor's former soldiers fought against Bourbon troops, the offshoot of which was an almost entirely bloodless revolution which swept a different style of monarch into power.

Louis-Philippe was from a different branch of the French royal family, descended from King Louis XIII. In 1789, to differentiate himself from King Louis XVI (and to save his head), Louis-Philippe had supported the Revolution, and had even served in the French Revolutionary army, helping to defeat the Prussians at Valmy in 1792. As a result, he had made a name for himself as a kind of 'people's royal', in much the same way as Napoleon wanted to be a 'people's emperor'. He had been forced into exile in England during the Terreur of 1793, but had never inspired the same hatred that revolutionaries and Bonapartists felt for Louis XVIII and Charles X, the brothers of the guillotined King Louis XVI.

Louis-Philippe was a supporter of constitutional monarchy, and did his best to soothe frayed tempers on all sides. Resisting countless insurrections and several waves of violent fighting, he consistently chose ministers who were known to be moderates, and even reinstated the revolutionary tricolour as the national flag.

This PR campaign worked, and Louis-Philippe became known as the *roi citoyen*, or citizen king. He turned the former royal palace of Versailles into a national museum, sent his sons to a state school in Paris, the Lycée Henri IV near the Panthéon (although then, as now, it was accessible only to the Parisian elite), and often walked around Paris dressed as a *bourgeois*, in an ordinary suit, with an umbrella under his arm.

Louis-Philippe's masterstroke, though, was to negotiate the return of Napoleon's remains from Saint Helena. Astutely putting national glory above sectarian politics, and banking on the hope that the French would unite around the memory of their former hero, he oversaw the completion of the Arc de Triomphe in 1836, commissioning frescoes for its façade in honour of Napoleon and all the armies that had fought for France between 1792 and 1815.*

---

* As a veteran of the Battle of Valmy, Louis-Philippe's own name was inscribed in the roll of honour.

The inauguration ceremony had to be cancelled because of a terrorist attack, but the gesture worked, and the novelist Honoré de Balzac wrote that when the Arc was complete, 'all hearts, even those hostile to the Emperor, said ardent prayers to heaven for the glory of the nation'.

Now all the Arc needed was for its instigator, Napoleon, to give it its final consecration. Louis-Philippe was understandably nervous about bringing back a political rival, albeit a dead one, but he went ahead and put in a request to the British for the return of Napoleon's remains. It was accepted immediately (the Brits had long since realised that the French were much too busy fighting among themselves to pose any military threat elsewhere), and in May 1840, French MPs voted to back what they called 'le retour des cendres', or 'the return of the ashes'.

Incidentally, one of the few parliamentary speeches against the idea was a brilliant one, given by the poet and politician Alphonse de Lamartine, who warned parliament to 'be careful in encouraging the notion that we must create a genius. I don't like men whose official doctrine is freedom, legality and progress, but whose symbols are the sword and despotism.' Before the debate began, Lamartine also said that 'the ashes [of Napoleon's career] have not gone out, and we are blowing on the sparks' – which was prophetic as well as poetic.

On 7 July 1840, a frigate left Toulon, the scene of Napoleon's first victory, for Saint Helena. Things were not as solemn as Napoleon himself would probably have liked: the ship was called the *Belle Poule* – the 'Beautiful Chicken', but also slang for a 'cute chick'. And en route for the South Atlantic, the crew (commanded by Louis-Philippe's twenty-one-year-old son François) stopped off in Bahia, Brazil, for two weeks of partying.

But the *Belle Poule* duly arrived in Saint Helena on 8 October, and handover of the remains was scheduled for the 15th, the twenty-fifth anniversary of Napoleon's arrival on the island. At midnight on the 14th, British soldiers began to dig, and after several hours, the coffins were raised and opened. Inside, Napoleon's body was found to be miraculously intact – French sources mention only that the nostrils were 'altered', the lips drawn back to reveal some teeth, and that there was a certain drying of the skin. Once death had been confirmed (after all, miracles do happen where martyrs are involved), the lead casket was re-sealed and placed inside two more coffins, made of ebony and oak. The whole funereal package now weighed some 1,200 kilos, and needed forty-three soldiers to lift it on to a carriage that a team of four horses was only just capable of pulling.

It took several hours to drag the coffins to the harbour and load them on to the *Belle Poule*, while the rain beat down and French cannons sounded a continuous salute for France's best-known artilleryman.

On 18 October, the ship set sail, and ran straight into trouble. Impossible as it seemed, Britain and France were practically at war again. The British had intervened to protect Syria against attack from Egypt, an ally of France, and old sabres were being retrieved from the Napoleonic cupboard and loudly rattled. The streets of Paris echoed to renewed cries of 'Guerre aux Anglais!' ('War on the English!'), no doubt louder because of the imminent return of *l'Empereur*.

The British Foreign Secretary, Lord Palmerston (who had rubber-stamped the return of Napoleon's remains), reminded the French that Britannia now ruled the waves, and declared that 'if France begins a war, she will to a certainty lose her ships, colonies and commerce' – he could of course have added 'remaining' in his sentence, and made things even more provocative. Privately, Palmerston also confided to colleagues that 'we ought to make up our mind to have war with France before many years have passed'. Here was one man for whom the Napoleonic Wars were far from over.

The crisis was, according to the above-mentioned sceptic Alphonse de Lamartine, 'the Waterloo of our diplomacy' – a timely reminder to his fellow French parliamentarians that Napoleonic idolatry was at least partly founded upon forgetfulness.

Meanwhile, thousands of miles away in the Atlantic, the *Belle Poule*, with its precious cargo, was terribly vulnerable to British attack, and young Prince François put the vessel on war alert, which mainly consisted of ordering the small crew to perform combat simulations, as though a few muskets could oppose a British warship.

In the event, the British did not commit the sacrilege of sending Napoleon to the bottom of the ocean, and the *Belle Poule* arrived safe and sound at Cherbourg on 30 November. From there, the coffins were sailed up the Seine to Paris, propelled by a wave of nostalgia. Everywhere there were aged veterans, their heads bowed in respect and remembrance, their old uniforms getting an airing after a quarter of a century in mothballs. The mood of national pomp and ceremony can be judged by the wealth of paintings and drawings depicting every inch of the body's progress.

In Paris, the coffins were placed on top of an enormous golden chariot pulled by twenty-four horses and accompanied by the flags of each of the *départements* (counties) Napoleon had created. The procession from the Pont de Neuilly on the Seine, through the Arc de Triomphe and across the river to the Invalides, his final resting place, was viewed by around a million spectators, inspiring Victor Hugo to gush:

May the people always keep you in their memory,
This day as beautiful as glory.

Paintings of the occasion don't show the freezing temperatures – it was around minus 10 degrees Celsius, so the size of the crowd was a real testament to Napoleon's pulling power. The Duchesse de Dino, a niece of the treacherous anti-Bonapartist diplomat Talleyrand, and no natural fan of Napoleon, wrote that the spectators were all moved by 'the exclusive memory of his victories that makes him so popular. Paris is declaring its desire for liberty, and with France humiliated by foreigners, it is celebrating the man who shackled this liberty.' The past was being filtered, and all whiff of defeat eliminated.

At the Invalides, the funeral cortège was greeted by a curious mix of weeping generals, diplomatically respectful royals (including Louis-Philippe) and badly behaved MPs, who chatted loudly, provoking Victor Hugo to remark that 'junior schoolchildren would have been spanked if they had behaved like these gentlemen in such a solemn place'.

As the coffin was laid to rest in the chapel, rumours were flying around France that it was empty, and that Napoleon was not really dead. He had returned from Saint Helena alive and well – aged seventy, younger than Blücher at the Battle of Waterloo. It would probably have taken a nineteenth-century version of Monty Python's blue parrot sketch to dampen the sentimentality: 'This emperor is no more. He has ceased to be. He has expired and gone to meet his maker. This is an ex-emperor.'

But even if Napoleon had in fact shuffled off his mortal coil and gone to meet the choir invisible, his spirit had returned, and it began causing chaos in France almost immediately.

VI

Far from consolidating Louis-Philippe's role as a unifying figure, the repatriation of Napoleon's body turned the King into an unexpected villain. Disgruntled voices were saying that the decision to sail the coffin up the Seine had been a political ploy designed to frustrate the general public, and that Louis-Philippe wanted to avoid a procession by road, through towns jammed with cheering Bonapartists, which would have reminded everyone how Napoleon had returned from Elba in 1815 to overthrow the monarchy. Worse, the news of the MPs' disrespect at the Invalides got out and shattered any illusions that Louis-Philippe's parliament was anything other than a gang of royalists.

A few months earlier, in August 1840, taking advantage of the upsurge of nostalgia, Louis-Napoléon – Bonaparte's nephew – had attempted a brief, and rather pathetic, invasion of France with a few soldiers, hoping to spark a mutiny in the army. He had been arrested, and had taken advantage of his trial to address the French people: 'You have served the cause, and you want to avenge the defeat.' The cause, of course, being Bonapartism, and the defeat, Waterloo. He was thrown into prison, where he occupied himself writing political pamphlets and sleeping with (female) servants, only to escape in 1846 by borrowing the clothes of a visiting artist.

In 1848, popular discontent with Louis-Philippe finally sparked a revolution, forcing the King to flee to England, disguised as a 'Mister Smith'.* Louis-Napoléon returned to France in triumph, stood for parliament (very much on the shoulders of his giant uncle) and was elected President. Then in 1851, he declared himself Emperor of France, just as the original Napoleon had done. One of his first acts was to create a new medal for the surviving veterans of the *Grande Armée* – the Médaille de Sainte-Hélène – a concrete reminder to the nation of his family's, and France's, past heroism.

Bonaparte was well and truly back, both in the physical

---

* For a full account of Louis-Philippe's farcical dash for safety, see my book *1000 Years of Annoying the French*.

form of the new Emperor Napoléon III* and in the towering ghost who had haunted France from his remote island since 1815, and who was now free to play poltergeist in the palaces he had once grabbed from both the royal family and the revolutionaries.

One question remains about the deceased Napoleon Bonaparte's return to France in 1840: why do the French refer to the repatriation of his partially decomposed body as *le retour des cendres*? After all, he was not cremated.

The *Larousse* French dictionary defines *cendres* as 'incombustible elements of a thing, which, after its combustion, remain in a powdery state', and as 'volcanic fragments of less than two millimetres projected by an eruption'. Neither of these definitions seems to fit.

Perhaps 'the return of the ashes' is just more elegant than 'the return of the body', which sounds coldly medical, or 'the return of the remains', which evokes putrefaction. But more than this, it seems to be about the difference between the physical Napoleon and his immortal, heroic spririt. Ashes are light, and as close as a body can get to abstraction (short of being blown to smithereens by one of Napoleon's cannons). Ashes are the essence of a dead person, almost like a powdered soul – and they will never decompose, thereby allowing everyone to remember the deceased in all the vigour of his or her youth.

---

* Napoléon II was Napoleon's young son, whom he named as his successor in 1815, but who was never crowned.

In this way, the decision by Bonapartists to refer to *cendres* is understandable, even if there were in fact no ashes. These are people who have what one might define as 'definition issues'. After all, they are the ones who define Waterloo as a 'defeat won by the British'. And their passion for redefining Napoleon has been growing ever since the so-called *cendres* were enshrined in what is still today the biggest and most-visited tomb in Paris.

7

~

CONSTRUCTING THE IDOL

'Tous voulaient lui parler, le toucher, l'entendre, au moins le
voir.'
'Everyone wanted to talk to him, touch him, hear him, or at
least see him.'

> – nineteenth-century French historian Georges
> Barral, describing how the Belgians welcomed
> Napoleon in June 1815

I

Modern Bonapartists have no intention of letting their
idolatry of Napoleon fade away. Every year the Fondation
Napoléon offers six grants of 7,500 euros to post-graduate
students writing a thesis on Napoleon. The Fondation
Napoléon is an organisation whose mission statement is to
'support the work of historians, to study Napoleonic history
and inform the general public about it, and to help preserve

and highlight Napoleonic heritage', so it is a pretty sure bet that subjects like 'Damage caused to the French economy by Napoleon's use of his conscripts as cannon fodder' or 'Trying to trace the lost artistic treasures looted by Napoleon's soldiers throughout his empire' probably won't receive a grant. And 7,500 euros may not sound very much, but French universities charge almost no tuition fees, so the grant represents about a year's rent for a student – a useful sum that also ensures the continued survival of Napoleon's glory.

Not that the foundation has much to worry about. There have always been plenty of volunteers willing to step forward and fire barrages of Bonapartist propaganda at a sceptical world.

Early anti-Napoleonic historians like Jean-Baptiste-Adolphe Charras failed to puncture the idolatry. Charras wrote in 1857 that the image of the betrayed, misunderstood hero was 'invented by the prisoner of Saint Helena, this Napoleon who spontaneously and sincerely converted to liberal ideas . . . who faithfully practised constitutional government . . . who only fell because of the accumulated errors of his lieutenants'.

One of the prime concerns of Bonapartist historians, starting with veterans of the Napoleonic army, has therefore been to document the most minor details of his life, and paint a portrait of the man behind the tough military façade. They have been spectacularly successful in documenting the countless gestures that point to Napoleon's profound, almost divine, goodness and love for humanity. In doing so, they are only obeying the Emperor's call to arms dictated to Las Cases on 1 May 1816: 'I have inspired every form of praise . . . pushed back the limits of glory! . . . Is there any attack against me that a historian could not rebuff?'

A prime example of the historians who have responded to the Emperor's call is Henry Houssaye, who in 1904 published a book called *Napoléon homme de guerre*. It paints a picture of a hero idolised by his men in a way no other general could aspire to. 'If Napoleon demanded a lot of his men, he preached by example,' Houssaye says. 'Whatever the weather, he never postponed a review of the troops. But the soldiers patiently endured rain heavy enough to fill rifle barrels with water because they saw their Emperor sitting motionless on his horse, without a coat, the rain flowing down his thighs.' An erotically charged piece of historical writing from a die-hard fan.

Houssaye tells many stories of Napoleon's human touch. Once, we learn, he went over to a group of soldiers who were drinking water out of a bucket. When all of them had drunk, he took the cup that they had used, and drank from it. An emperor drinking from the same cup as mere footsoldiers? It was like Jesus washing his disciples' feet, *n'est-ce pas?*

On another occasion, Houssaye tells us, Napoleon ordered a surgeon to continue operating on ordinary soldiers rather than go and save a wounded general: 'Your duty is to all men, not to one.' Houssaye admits that Napoleon might have been overdoing his democratic act for an audience, but adds that 'even so, he was an actor with the whole of Europe for a theatre, twenty nations as his audience, half a million soldiers to applaud him and, to protect his memory, the long succession of centuries'.

Other historians underline the fierce devotion Napoleon inspired in his men because of his obvious love for them. A much-recounted anecdote is the story of how, at 2.30 p.m. on 15 June 1815,* after his dash to Belgium, Napoleon arrived at Charleroi dead tired, and fell asleep on a chair in the courtyard of a farm. Marching past, some of his soldiers saw the Emperor and applauded even the act of sleeping. Some part of Napoleon's sleeping brain seemed to notice that the soldiers were slowing down their advance to look at him and, without opening his eyes, he waved them on. The historian Jean-Claude Damamme sees this as proof that the Emperor's brain never rested, that he was totally focused on defending France, though a more cynical observer might suggest that Napoleon had simply been trying to wave away the noisy rabble that was disturbing his Corsican siesta.

In historical accounts presenting Napoleon as a tragic hero, the observations naturally get more acute the closer he gets to Waterloo. As he rode among his men on the morning of 18 June 1815, infantrymen hoisted their tall fur hats on their bayonets, cavalrymen lifted their helmets on the tips of their swords, and they all shouted 'Vive l'Empereur!' (not, we are meant to notice, 'Vive la France!').

When Napoleon inspected troops on his white mare

---

* These anecdotes from Napoleon's life are very often timed and dated to the minute.

Marie,* an officer noted that 'never has "Vive l'Empereur!" been shouted with more enthusiasm. It was like madness.'

By contrast, French historians like to stress that Wellington's men were merely silent and respectful. 'He was their general,' Jean-Claude Damamme tells us, 'not their idol.' Not only this, Napoleon was such a good guy that British soldiers who came into contact with him, or even saw him, fell under his spell. In Chapter 5 we saw the effect of Napoleon's charisma on the sailors aboard the *Bellerophon*. They were of course reacting to the star quality of the famous general, but French historians tell many stories of Napoleon's kindness towards his enemies.

On one occasion, for example, some British prisoners of war were made to rebuild a broken bridge over the River Meuse so that Napoleon could cross without getting his boots wet. To show his gratitude, Napoleon offered them all a sniff from his personal snuffbox, and then had them freed.

Another time, Napoleon, ensconced in his army camp at Boulogne, vainly hoping that he would be able to cross the Channel and invade England, heard that someone else had almost beaten him to it. A young English sailor, who had escaped from capitivity in France, had been hiding in the woods near Boulogne. Almost starved to death and completely

---

* Napoleon had several horses, more than one of them white. He rode Marie on the morning of 18 June to inspect his troops, before switching to the more famous Marengo during the battle. Marengo was wounded and left at Napoleon's billet, the farmhouse at Le Caillou. Marie was also at Le Caillou when it was captured by the Prussians, and Blücher returned the white mare to the German stud farm from which Napoleon had 'requisitioned' her in 1813.

naked, he had been caught trying to set off for England in a makeshift raft. Napoleon asked to see the lad, and was touched by his plea that he wanted to go home and see his sick mother. Even if it was a made-up sob story, Napoleon ordered his men to give the sailor clothes and money, and send him back to England.

Napoleon even extended his clemency to the hated Prussians. After the Battle of Ligny on 16 June 1815, at which 12,000 French and 20,000 Prussians fell, dead or wounded, he came across a group of Prussian casualties who were not being cared for. He immediately gave orders for them to be issued with brandy. How many wounded men this sudden dose of alcohol killed has not been recorded, but Napoleon was presumably working on the basis that what doesn't kill you makes you stronger. In any case, a story about kindness to Prussians, when everyone knew of their murderous cruelty to French casualties after Waterloo and their call for Napoleon to be executed, only makes him seem more Christ-like. It was a case of turning the other cheek and waiting for a Prussian sword to slash it.

There are countless tales of Napoleon's excellent relations with the Belgians in June 1815, a fully reciprocated love that Bonapartist historians cite in order to give legitimacy to his campaign, the aim of which was not only to defend his own regime but to liberate Belgium from foreign (as opposed to French) occupation. Not that the Belgians had much choice. As Napoleon once told a French farmer, 'Les Belges sont des Français' ('Belgians are French').

As he crossed the country in his carriage, en route for

Ligny and Waterloo, we are often told that Napoleon was hailed by Belgian civilians. The nineteenth-century French historian Georges Barral says that 'everyone wanted to talk to him, touch him, hear him, or at least see him'. Father-like, Napoleon responded kindly: 'Thank you, my children, thank you, but keep out of the way because today or tomorrow there will be a great battle here.' Barral concludes the scene by telling us that 'they scattered his route with flowers, among them many red poppies that looked like splashes of blood'. (Bonapartist writers are very fond of these poetic, prophetic touches that add to the legend of the tragic hero.)

Wherever he went in Belgium, despite the colossal weight of worry on his shoulders, Napoleon stopped to chat, producing banalities that are quoted in memoirs as though they were pearls of wisdom distributed by a visiting god. In a small village near Charleroi, he asked a priest, 'Monsieur l'Abbé, do you plan to end your days here in Jamioulx?' The old clergyman replied, 'Yes, Sire, life is very pleasant here.' A touching exchange just before a monstrous battle, perhaps, but surely no more meaningful than the Queen asking, 'Did you bake these cakes yourself?'

After the battle, the Belgians repaid this debt to their French godfather by harbouring wounded Napoleonic soldiers and giving them civilian clothes. They did this at considerable risk to their own personal safety. As Pierre Alexandre Fleury de Chaboulon, who was Napoleon's private secretary until Waterloo, wrote in his memoirs, 'defying the anger of the ferocious Prussians, they [the Belgians] came out of their homes to point out escape routes and direct us through the enemy columns'.

And all this for love of Napoleon . . .

II

Napoleon once said admiringly of himself, 'What a novel my life has been.' It might have been a touch more arrogant, but much truer, if he had said, 'What a lot of novels my life will be. And quite a few poems too.' Because it is not only Bonapartist historians and anonymous Belgians who have ensured Napoleon's enduring image as a hero. Both during his lifetime and since his death, Napoleon has attracted the attention of some very big-name literary admirers.

First among them are, naturally, the French.

Stendhal, author of the classic romantic novel *Le Rouge et le Noir*, published in 1830, was a huge fan. As a young man he was an officer in Napoleon's army (albeit more of an organiser than a combatant), and even took part in the disastrous Russian campaign. Nevertheless, he emerged from the ice and snow as a Bonapartist, and when Napoleon's empire came to an end, he emigrated from France rather than stay on in a country that had scorned its greatest hero.

Stendhal wrote two essays about Napoleon's life, giving space to the errors as well as the achievements: he thought, for example, that the pompous coronation ceremony in 1804 was 'absurd', and that Napoleon's attitude to politics was 'despotic', but that overall, Bonaparte was 'one of the greatest men since Caesar, and in my opinion he surpassed him'. This was from a man who caught syphilis while on service in Italy, and who only just managed to cross the frozen River Berezina with his life – proving once again that those who served with Napoleon were willing to forgive him anything, apparently out of gratitude for letting them come along for the ride.

Stendhal paid Napoleon the ultimate literary tribute. In *Le Rouge et le Noir*, Stendhal makes his main character, Julien Sorel, one of the great romantic heroes of French literature, a Napoleon fan. The narrator tells us that 'Julien hardly spent an hour of his life without thinking that Bonaparte, a poor young lieutenant, had made himself master of the world with his sword alone.' Julien seems to forget the hundreds of thousands of men who gave their lives during the Emperor's battles, but then romantic heroes – like Bonapartists – rarely have a detached view of the facts.

Someone who was more aware of the human cost of the Napoleonic saga, but no less of an admirer, was Honoré de Balzac, one of the most prolific novelists ever. The ninety-three books of his *Comédie Humaine* cycle, begun in 1829, chronicle the whole of early nineteenth-century France, starting just after Waterloo.

There are veterans of the *Grande Armée* in several of Balzac's novels, and Napoleon makes two personal appearances, in *La Vendetta* (a *Romeo and Juliet*-like tragedy about warring Corsican families) and *Une Ténébreuse Affaire* ('A Dark Affair'), a crime story about a royalist anti-Napoleon plot. In the latter book, a woman goes to Jena in Germany, where Napoleon is preparing for battle, and begs the Emperor to spare the plotters' lives, insisting that they are innocent. Balzac gives Napoleon a wonderful line in reply – he points to his soldiers and says, 'They are certainly innocent, but tomorrow, 30,000 will be dead.'

It was a highly credible quip that highlights Balzac's only reservation about Napoleon – the endless bloodshed. In everything else, Balzac aspired to be a Napoleonic figure. He had a statue of *l'Empereur* in his study, inscribed with the motto 'What he achieved with the sword, I will accomplish with the pen'.* Balzac seriously saw himself as a literary Napoleon, comparing the all-embracing scale of his writing with the Emperor's more physical endeavours. He wrote that 'Ideas set off like the battalions of the *Grande Armée* . . . Memories charge forward, their standards deployed; the light cavalry of similes breaks into a magnificent gallop; the artillery of logic moves up with its weapons and powder charges; attacks of wit advance as skirmishers . . . The paper is covered with ink as the conflict begins and ends with torrents of black liquid, just like a battle with its black gunpowder. Every day is a Battle of Austerlitz of creation.'

Despite the playful exaggeration, Balzac almost certainly meant his army of metaphors to be taken seriously. After all, he was a French novelist.

*

* This was probably a reaction to the famous quotation 'the pen is mightier than the sword', which comes from the play *Richelieu*, by Edward Bulwer-Lytton, first performed in 1839. Bulwer-Lytton was well known throughout Europe and his plays were translated into French.

However, as we have already seen, the greatest of Napoleon's French literary fans, and the one with the keenest sense of Napoleon's place at the heart of history, was also arguably the grandest figure in nineteenth-century French literature – Victor Hugo. The son of a Napoleonic general, Joseph Léopold Sigisbert Hugo, and a royalist mother, young Victor's parents separated because of their political differences. He went to live with his mother, and his first poems were pro-royalist. In one of them, published in 1822, he went so far as to describe Napoleon as a 'living plague'. Napoleon had in fact just died, but it was clearly a case of poetic licence.

Hugo's mother also died around the same time as the Emperor she hated, and as Hugo grew closer to his father, he began to express pride at being the son of a Napoleonic veteran. In 1823 he published a poem in honour of the Arc de Triomphe, the monument to Napoleon's victories, when Louis XVIII was thinking of having the arch completed. It lists the Emperor's glories, and ends with a strange (but no doubt well-meaning) line that seems to hint at Napoleon's diminutive height: 'May the giant of our glory be able to pass through without bending down.'

A few years later in 1829, in a poem called 'Lui' ('Him'), Hugo summed up Napoleon's role in history: 'You dominate our age, no matter if it is as angel or demon.' And he went on to publish several more poems that were almost entirely positive about Napoleon and his empire. In 1840, when Napoleon's remains finally arrived back in France, Hugo even wrote an elegy in which he referred to Waterloo as 'the false-hood of a victory'.

This admiration led Hugo to be one of the foremost campaigners in favour of a return to power for the Bonaparte family in 1848. But when Louis-Napoléon, nephew of the first Napoleon, failed to deliver the democracy he had promised, and then declared himself Emperor Napoléon III, Hugo began making speeches comparing the sadly departed 'Napoléon le Grand' with the new upstart 'Napoléon le Petit' (yet another unfortunate height reference), and in 1851 he was forced into exile in the Channel Islands.

While in exile, Hugo wrote his greatest works about Waterloo. In his poem 'L'Expiation' (meaning 'penitence', or, for those who use the word in English, 'expiation'), he invented one of the Napoleonic sayings that has entered the French language. If someone says of a town, a café or a dull party that 'c'est morne plaine', they mean it's as dead as a doornail. This comes from Hugo's famous line in 'L'Expiation': 'Waterloo, Waterloo, Waterloo, morne plaine', meaning that the battle, so bad he named it thrice, took place on a 'mournful plain'.

Not that it would have been mournful if Napoleon had won, because Hugo also claims in the poem that 'victory followed this man everywhere', and that it really should have accompanied Napoleon to Belgium. As we saw in Chapter 2, Hugo even suggests that God was at Waterloo, and that it was there that He ultimately decided Napoleon was simply too big a hero for the good of the planet. Even so, the poem explains that this didn't mean that God was an anti-Bonapartist. As his soldiers flee the battlefield, Napoleon appeals directly to heaven:

My empire has been smashed like glass.
I am beaten, my soldiers are dead!
Is this a punishment, God, that you bring down on my
head?
Then above the cries and the rumble of cannon fire
He heard a voice that answered: *Non!**

'L'Expiation' does an excellent job of publicising the glorious version of the battle that Napoleon dictated in his memoirs. As darkness fell, Hugo wrote, Napoleon 'almost had victory', and Wellington was 'pinned up against a forest'. But then triumph slipped out of Napoleon's grasp, abandoning him like a deserting soldier: 'Tu désertais, victoire'. It is almost as if Hugo assumed that victory owed its allegiance to the French army. The tragic heroes of the poem, and the battle, are of course the *Garde Impériale*, 'regiments of granite and steel' that march forward fearlessly only to melt in the furnace of British cannon fire.

All in all, 'L'Expiation' is a masterpiece of hero worship that has coloured French memories of Waterloo just as strongly as Shakespeare did when he immortalised Agincourt in *Henry V* – the difference being, of course, that Hugo was idolising the losers.

The idolatry was sincerely meant, and the battle scenes are brilliantly written, even though Hugo didn't actually visit the 'morne plaine' himself until several years after he

---

* It is best to leave God's answer in its original form, because He was obviously speaking French at the time.

wrote 'L'Expiation'. He felt that the wound was too fresh in his, and France's, memory to be probed so directly. Hugo finally plucked up the courage to go to Waterloo in May 1861, for the fortieth anniversary of Napoleon's death, when he took up residence in a hotel on the battlefield and, as he put it, 'performed the autopsy on the catastrophe. I spent two months bent over the corpse.'

During his mournful months in Belgium, Hugo finished off the text of his great five-volume historical novel *Les Misérables*, adding details to the long chapter on Waterloo that he had already written.

As we have already seen, in *Les Misérables* Hugo turned Waterloo into a glorious moral victory. In doing so, he also managed to set in literary stone the image that Bonapartists still carry in their hearts today (and express in countless books, articles and talks). Hugo does in many ways the opposite of the job that Shakespeare did for England's Richard III. Until very recently, almost everyone in Britain thought that Richard was nothing more than an evil hunchback, whereas in fact he was an enlightened king who, for example, ensured that laws were written in English rather than Latin so that ordinary people could understand them. In a similar way, Hugo describes the sheer greatness of Napoleon and his regime in a way that makes it practically impossible for a French reader to resist feeling an upsurge of patriotic nostalgia. He has the character of Marius exclaim that 'To be the empire of such an emperor, what a splendid destiny for a nation, when that nation is France and it adds its genius to the genius of that man!' *Vive la France*, indeed.

In *Les Misérables*, Hugo also expresses the slight sense of paranoia that has crept into French patriotism in the past couple of centuries, the feeling that everyone is against them: 'What was Waterloo? A victory? No, a lottery won by Europe and paid for by France.' Hugo could almost be describing France's attitude to the European Union today.

Hugo also makes a startling comparison between the reserved Wellington and the more artistic, expressive Napoleon. Waterloo was a battle, Hugo says, between British 'precision, planning, geometry, prudence, a safe line of retreat, well-managed reserves, stubborn calm . . . nothing left to chance' and Napoleon's very French 'intuition, feeling . . . superhuman instinct, flamboyant vision . . . prodigious art and scornful impetuosity, all the mysteriousness of a profound soul'.

Hugo could almost be comparing Margaret Thatcher and Eric Cantona. It is a self-image of flamboyant France that still goes down well with the French today.

All in all, this message at the heart of Hugo's greatest novel is simple: Waterloo turned Napoleon, and thereby the French spirit, into the very essence of heroism. Hugo sums it up, as usual, in a very quotable quote: 'Defeat increased the stature of the vanquished. Napoleon fallen looked bigger than Napoleon standing.' (And that was almost certainly not a height-related joke.)

To be fair to Hugo, he did temper his out-and-out hero worship of France's greatest warlord with a touch of compassion. He wrote, for example, that 'Waterloo was more of a massacre than a battle', and expressed the hope that the slaughter on all sides had achieved something: 'While Napoleon was dying at Longwood, the sixty thousand men who fell on the battlefield at Waterloo were peacefully putrefying, and something of their peace spread across the world.'

In *Les Misérables*, Hugo also gave us one of the most vivid pieces of anti-war writing ever put to paper by someone who never fought. It must have been inspired by standing on the battlefield and imagining the last moments of one of the soldiers: 'There is something terrifying here, a reality that breaks through the dream: to live, to see the sun, to be in full possession of virile life, to laugh out loud, to run towards glory, to feel in your chest a lung that breathes, a heart that beats, a will that reasons, to speak, think, hope, love, have a mother, a wife, children, to see light and then suddenly, in the space of a single cry, to fall into darkness, to tumble, roll over, crush, be crushed, to glimpse the corn stalks, the flowers, the leaves, the branches, but be unable to hold on to anything, to realise that your sword is useless, to feel men beneath you, horses on top of you, to struggle in vain, your bones smashed by the kick of a horse, a hoof squashing the eyes out of your head, to bite furiously into a horseshoe, to suffocate, shout, twist, be buried, and to say to yourself: just a moment ago I was alive!'

Nonetheless, the overriding theme in Hugo's Napoleonic writings, like that of Stendhal and Balzac, is that Napoleon was a figure whom the French should be proud to venerate for the rest of time.

And these Bonaparte fans weren't the only ones to be

broadcasting the message. The last word on Napoleon's place in nineteenth-century French literature has to go to an unlikely source – the nobleman Viscount François-René Chateaubriand (1768–1848), an ardent royalist whose cousin was shot in 1809 for anti-Bonapartist activities. In his most famous work, *Mémoires d'Outre-Tombe* ('Memoirs from Beyond the Grave'), Chateaubriand pays Napoleon a back-handed but highly prescient compliment: 'The world belongs to Napoleon. That which the destroyer could not conquer, his reputation usurps. When alive he lost the world; dead, he possesses it.'

III

Unsurprisingly, Britain's most feared enemy also inspired some of its most famous writers. Napoleon's greatest English-language publicist in the early nineteenth century was Sir Walter Scott, author of historical novels like *Rob Roy* and *Ivanhoe*, who in 1827 published *The Life of Napoleon Buonaparte, Emperor of the French* – nine volumes and more than a million words long.

Scott was of course a Scot, and might have been naturally inclined to feel sympathetic towards a Frenchman – Auld Alliance *oblige*. But as the use of the Italian form of Napoleon's name in the title suggests, Scott was not a French-style Napoleon fan. His book is as obsessively detailed as any Bonapartist history book, but a lot more balanced. Throughout, he is just as liable to lambast Napoleon for his despotism ('his system of government . . . aimed at the subjugation of the world') as he is to praise the man for his 'patriotic attention to the public welfare' of France. And as we saw in Chapter 6, Scott takes a strictly impartial line when discussing Napoleon's 'persecution' at the hands of his jailer, Sir Hudson Lowe.

For the modern reader, the book's attention to detail is hard going, just as it must have been for most people in the 1820s. How many nineteenth-century Brits would have been fascinated to learn, for example, the exact responsibilities of Napoleon's Legislative Body, or its precise relationship to his Tribunate and Council of State?

Even some of the dramatic scenes in Napoleon's career make for unusual reading because they are treated with such resounding neutrality. In 1814, for example, when Napoleon crosses France after his *adieux* at Fontainebleau, Scott notes drily that 'cries of *vive l'Empereur*' were frequently heard, but that in some places people 'insulted his passage with shouts of *vive le Roi*'. The whole episode feels curiously undramatic, like a no-score draw.

But elsewhere, Scott's moral judgements shine through the mass of neutrally reported historical detail. He understands – but still criticises – Napoleon's tantrums on Saint Helena. He also disapproves of Napoleon's talent for self-deception, and before describing the Battle of Waterloo, he huffs that 'Napoleon's extravagant speculations [that Britain would stop fighting him if they lost there] can only serve to show how very little he must have known of the English nation'.

Scott pours scorn on early Bonapartist accounts of the battle: 'The French authors have pretended, that [English] squares were broken, and colours taken, but this assertion, upon the unified testimony of every British officer present, is a positive untruth.' (And who is going to doubt the word of a British officer against a few Frenchies, what?)

Scott's insistence that the truth be told forces him to smash some especially sacred French idols. When describing the final stand of the *Vieille Garde*, he rubbishes the 'fictions' that have been 'industriously circulated by the friends of Napoleon' about Cambronne defying the English and saying that the *Garde* preferred to die rather than surrender. Scott even denies that Cambronne did anything particularly heroic: he simply 'gave up his own sword, and remained prisoner'. He also dismisses the notion that the *Vieille Garde* were determined to die, saying that it would be absurd to glorify them for 'an act of regimental suicide'.

As for Napoleon's own account of the battle, in which he heaped all the blame on his generals, Scott calls it 'a mere military romance, full of gratuitous suppositions'. He says that Napoleon and his apologists 'concur in a very futile attempt to excuse the defeat at Waterloo', and that 'it has been a favourite assertion with almost all the French, and some English writers, that the English were on the point of being defeated, when the Prussian force came up. The contrary is the truth.'

Clearly, Scott didn't write a million-word biography because he was a Napoleon fan. In fact, he chose his subject because he and his publisher thought that history's most famous Frenchman would sell books. This was a tale of blood and thunder, ending in the most celebrated British

victory since Agincourt, and it earned Scott more than
£10,000 – a fortune in those days. But Scott was interested
in more than money – despite Napoleon's moral weaknesses,
Scott constantly reminds us that he was an exceptional
human being compared to those, including Scott himself,
'whose steps have never led them beyond the middle path
in life'.

Predictably, Scott's criticism of Napoleon's character
faults infuriated Bonapartists when the book came out. One
of Napoleon's *compagnons d'exil*, General Gaspard Gourgaud,
published a virulent *Réfutation des calomnies de la vie de
Napoléon par Walter Scott*. But overall, Scott's criticisms
only seem to have galvanised Bonapartist historians in their
determination to deify their idol. Ever since his million-
word cannonade was published, they have mounted their
own last stand to perpetuate the legend of Cambronne's
tragic heroes, and the idea that Napoleon beat Wellington
before the Prussians finally showed up. And Scott's biography is often cited, if not quoted at length, in Bonapartist
histories of Napoleon's life. After all, anyone who merits
nine volumes of English prose must be a hero, *n'est-ce pas*?

IV

Sir Walter Scott was in his fifties when he wrote his
biography of Napoleon. He was an old-school, moralistic
historian, a kind of Scottish judge whose book was a nine-
volume summing up, leaning towards a guilty verdict.
Napoleon had to rely on a younger, more Romantic, British

soul for French-style idolisation: and this he received in both word and deed from England's most famous – or infamous – poet of the time, Lord Byron.

As a schoolboy at Harrow at the turn of the nineteenth century, Byron was fired up with Bonapartist bravado, and kept a bust of the all-conquering Napoleon in his study. At the time, such an unpatriotic gesture must have been very daring, a bit like putting a poster of the Sex Pistols on your bedroom wall in 1976.

When Napoleon lost at Leipzig in 1813, the adult Byron wrote in his diary: 'Oh my head! – how it aches! – the horrors of digestion! I wonder how Buonaparte's dinner agrees with him?'

Understandably, his digestion was even more disturbed when Napoleon abdicated in 1814, and it looked as though he had tamely given up the fight. In 'Ode to Napoleon Buonaparte', Byron wrote about his former hero with the pain of a disappointed fan:

A lion in the conquering hour!
In wild defeat a hare!
Thy mind hath vanished with thy power,
For Danger brought despair.
The dreams of sceptres now depart,
And leave thy desolated heart
The Capitol of care!
Dark Corsican, 'tis strange to trace
Thy long deceit and last disgrace.

However, after Napoleon's dramatic escape from Elba in 1815, Byron changed his tune again, and was with his idol in spirit at Waterloo, unlike most of his fellow Englishmen. Instead of indulging in patriotic triumphalism, on 15 July 1815 Byron wrote 'Napoleon's Farewell', in the defeated Emperor's own voice, sagely predicting that France would miss him sorely. The sentiments in the poem are almost French:

> I have warr'd with a world which vanquish'd me only
> When the meteor of conquest allured me too far . . .
> Farewell to thee, France! When thy diadem crown'd me,
> I made thee the gem and the wonder of earth . . .
> The violet* still grows in the depth of thy valleys;
> Though withered, thy tears will unfold it again.

In 1816, accused in England of sodomy and incest, Byron fled to the continent, vowing to model himself on Napoleon and become a pan-European traveller and warrior. He was self-aware, though, and admitted that 'With me there is, as Napoleon said, but one step between the sublime and the ridiculous.'** True to his word, Byron had an absurdly de luxe version of Napoleon's captured carriage made, and travelled in it to Brussels, Geneva and on to Italy. The carriage was kitted out with facsimiles of Napoleon's travel bed, his portable library, and even his dining utensils. It was enormous, requiring between four and six horses to pull it, and cost £500

---

* Napoleon's favourite flower, and his emblem.
** This phrase is one of Napoleon's inventions. He once said that 'du sublime au ridicule, il n'y a qu'un pas' ('there is only one step').

– approximately fifteen times the annual salary of the men who made it. Or rather, it would have cost £500, but Byron never paid the bill. Perhaps it was only poetic justice, as well as its excessive weight, that made the carriage break down three times before it even got to Brussels. Byron eventually reached Waterloo, and hired a Cossack horse to tour the battlefield. This was only a year after the battle and the atmosphere must have been eerie to say the least. The third canto of Byron's famous poem *Childe Harold's Pilgrimage*, written in 1816, was partly inspired by the visit. He opens it with a stark anti-British, anti-royalist, line inspired by arriving at the hallowed battlefield: 'Stop – for thy tread is on Empire's dust!'

Byron was horrified at the number of deaths caused by Britain and its allies in their determination to do away with Napoleon and reinstate the royalists on the French throne. He had lost one of his cousins at Waterloo, and described the horrors of battle in heart-rending terms:

The earth is covered thick with other clay,
Which her own clay shall cover, heaped and pent,
Rider and horse, – friend, foe, – in one red burial blent!

When Byron visited the battlefield, there must still have been human remains in open view. No one could have collected, buried or ploughed over all those human fragments. Byron's cousin, Major Frederick Howard, was one of the casualties whose grave could be identified, and he was eventually dug up and repatriated to England.

Despite the horrors, Byron indulged in some souvenir

shopping, acquiring a breastplate, a plumed helmet and a sword, then continued his tour of Europe on a decidedly Napoleonic theme. Near Milan he saw a partially built Arc de Triomphe in honour of Napoleon's victories, and wrote that it was 'so beautiful as to make one regret its non-completion'. And on Isola Bella, in Lago Maggiore, he visited the laurel tree on which, a few days before the Battle of Marengo in 1800, Napoleon had carved, with impeccable Italian spelling, the word 'Battaglia' (battle).

Incidentally, some sixty years later that same tree and its still-visible graffiti was visited by Edward Bulwer-Lytton, the man who first said that the pen was mightier than the sword, who was far less Bonapartist than Byron. He wrote a poem that includes the verse:

Now, year by year, the warrior's iron mark
Crumbles away from the majestic tree
The indignant life-sap ebbing from the bark
Where the grim death-word to humanity
Profaned the Lord of Day.

Byron, on the other hand, remained a staunch fan of the man who defaced trees, and even began signing himself with Napoleon's initials 'NB' – for Noel Byron – after taking the name of his mother-in-law in a bid to inherit her wealth.

He also amassed a collection of Napoleonic memorabilia that, if put up for auction today, would pay off any bankrupt poet's debts. He bought, among other things, a lock of

Napoleon's hair, imperial notepaper, snuffboxes featuring Napoleon's portrait, gold coins struck by Napoleon's mint, a Napoleon cameo pin, and he even put in an unsuccessful offer for Napoleon's coronation robes, which came up for sale in London, and would have made a wonderful travelling outfit for the roving English rake.

Right up until his death in 1824, while fighting to liberate Greece from Turkish rule, Byron was turning out pro-Bonapartist lines. In a letter sent from Italy in 1821 he wrote of his scorn for British politicians since the fall of Napoleon: 'Since that period, we have been the slaves of fools.' And in the ninth canto of his poem *Don Juan*, written between 1822 and 1823, he poured scorn on Wellington himself, ironically asking the Iron Duke:

And I shall be delighted to learn who,
Save you and yours, have gained by Waterloo?

A poem called 'Age of Bronze' provides Byron's final word on the battle, and sounds very French in the way it toes the line set out in Napoleon's memoirs, which were published, like this poem, in 1823:

Oh, bloody and most bootless Waterloo!
Which proves how fools may have their fortune too,
Won half by blunder, half by treachery.

Napoleon couldn't have put it better himself.

V

Bizarrely for a man who spent much of his career fighting Prussia, Napoleon also had admirers among the Germans, especially philosophers who were attracted to the Frenchman's 'man of action' image.

Georg Hegel, one of the founders of modern European philosophy, was fascinated by the French Revolution, which he saw as the first time that individuals had achieved true political freedom in European society (he probably hadn't noticed all the individuals who were being imprisoned, decapitated or conscripted at the time). And when, on the day before the Battle of Jena in October 1806, Hegel watched Napoleon and his men march into the town of Jena, he wrote excitedly to a friend as though he had seen the embodiment of this new French freedom: 'I saw the Emperor – this world soul – riding around the city, reconnoitring. It is a truly wonderful feeling to see such an individual, who, sitting on his horse, is entirely focused on one point, embracing the whole world, and dominating it.'

Napoleon certainly dominated Jena – his men were billeted in Hegel's own house and Hegel himself was forced to leave the town and get a job 200 kilometres away in Bamberg. But he seems to have borne his eviction with true philosophical stoicism, because he adopted Napoleon as the model for his notion of the soul or mind at the heart of history, acutely and uniquely conscious of the 'end purpose' of events, and shaping them accordingly.

Napoleon, like a select few emperors and conquerors before him, was admirable, Hegel thought, because they alone knew 'the truth of their times and of their worlds'. They were, Hegel said, 'aware of historical necessity: which is why, like Alexander the Great and Caesar, Napoleon is a wise man – he knows the true nature of his era'.

Like Alexander and Caesar, Napoleon also acted upon this knowledge: according to Hegel, he knew 'what is necessary and what to do when the time comes'. He was a man of action, not a mere thinker; he *was* what he *did*. Hegel saw Napoleon as an 'instrument of the Absolute', affirming human power over the flux of history.

All this applied perfectly while Napoleon was enjoying success, of course. Once he was ousted from power, the theory that the French superman was imposing himself on history seemed to collapse somewhat. When Napoleon abdicated in 1814, Hegel decreed that it was 'a tremendous genius destroying himself. It is the most tragic thing ever.' But, undeterred, Hegel also explained that Napoleon was doomed to fall (like the murdered Caesar and the probably poisoned Alexander) because, as an instrument of the Absolute, he was vulnerable to the greater necessities of history. This dovetails nicely with Victor Hugo's view that Napoleon was just too big for the nineteenth century to cope with, and that God (that is, the Christian Absolute) had decided it was time for Napoleon's reign to end.

And just like Stendhal, who suffered terribly while serving *l'Empereur* but went on to idolise him, Hegel, the man who lost his home to French invaders, forgave Napoleon, and founded a whole philosophy of history on him, elevating him to the pantheon of immortal heroes.

This heroic status was confirmed by the inventor of the superman, Friedrich Nietzsche, the German with the hugest moustache in the history of philosophy.

In 1882, Nietzsche published a book called *Fröhliche Wissenschaft*, which was originally translated as *Gay Science* but which might be better rendered these days as *Joyous Knowledge*, to avoid misconceptions.* This was a series of essays and poems on power, in which Nietzsche praised Napoleon, describing him as a mixture of *Unmensch* (inhuman) and an *Übermensch* (superman).

Nietzsche thought that Napoleon's greatness lay in his ability to transcend the boundaries of mere nationalism – like many Germans at the end of the nineteenth century, Nietzsche was obsessed by his country's recent evolution into a nation, after centuries of being a collection of tiny princedoms. Nietzsche especially admired Napoleon's vision of 'one Europe, which was to be mistress of the world', and said that he was 'the only *Mensch* strong enough' to achieve this goal.

Nietzsche also credited Napoleon with inventing a modern era of scientific warfare and of total war, while being soundly rooted in ancient values. Like some Greek colossus, Napoleon was, Nietzsche thought, a 'block of granite'

* Nietzsche's original German title was inspired by a Provençal concept of *gai saber* and, like the French word *savoir*, *saber* means 'knowledge'.

against the weakness of the modern world, and that he had, for a short time at least, 'virilised Europe'.

These were the kinds of ideas that made Nietzsche so popular with his own countrymen a few decades later, when they were preparing their own bid to become mistresses (or rather, masters) of Europe. Not that any Bonapartists would countenance for an instant a comparison between Hitler – genocidal maniac trying to impose his world view on Europe by means of the latest tank and aeroplane technology – and Napoleon – heroic visionary trying to impose his world view on Europe by means of the latest artillery technology. Absolutely no similarity at all.

Nietzsche also alleged that Johann Wolfgang von Goethe's Faust, the most famous character in all German drama, a kind of Teutonic Hamlet, was influenced by Napoleon. Here, Nietzsche seems to have gone too far: Goethe actually met Napoleon in Erfurt in October 1808, but didn't take the opportunity to flatter the French Emperor by informing him that he had a starring role in German literature. Instead, during their conversation Napoleon managed to browbeat the seventy-year-old Goethe into admitting that certain parts of his youthful novel *The Sorrows of Young Werther* were 'not natural', and then informed Germany's greatest dramatist that tragedy had nothing to do with destiny. Destiny, Napoleon said, was controlled by politics. Goethe quickly asked if he could be excused.

While on the subject of Germans, it would be a mistake to forget Beethoven, a composer who was highly influenced by current affairs. His opera *Fidelio*, first performed in 1805, was based on a French revolutionary play about a political prisoner; and in 1804 Beethoven dedicated a symphony to Napoleon – his third, the *Eroica*. The original manuscript bears the title 'Buonaparte', because Beethoven was a fervent admirer of the young Napoleon, whom he, like Hegel, saw as the embodiment of French democracy.

Beethoven later withdrew the dedication, and some Bonapartists would like us to believe that it was simply so that he could replace it with the name of the man who was paying him, the Bohemian Prince Franz Joseph von Lobkowitz. However, the truth is that when Napoleon declared himself Emperor of France, Beethoven was furious and shouted that the Frenchman had become a petty tyrant: 'He is nothing but an ordinary mortal! Now he is going to trample on everyone's rights just to appease his ambitions.' The great composer immediately walked over to his desk, ripped up the title sheet with the 'Buonaparte' dedication and replaced it with 'Eroica'.

Nevertheless, Beethoven later admitted that he had written the work for the idealistic revolutionary general that Napoleon had originally been, and when the score was first printed in 1806, it bore an Italian inscription saying that the symphony had been composed 'in memory of a great man'. Beethoven was contributing to Napoleonic nostalgia before the Frenchman had even been deposed.

By comparison, Europe's most famous composer of the time almost forgot Wellington completely. To celebrate the Englishman's victory over the French army at Vitoria in 1813,

Beethoven wrote just a fifteen-minute work called *Wellingtons Sieg* ('Wellington's Victory'). And poor old Blücher got nothing.

Beethoven was fairly typical of the artistic community in nineteenth-century Europe, especially its more Romantic, visionary members. In terms of cultural immortality, for Beethoven as well as a whole flock of famous European writers, only one of the protagonists at Waterloo was the winner.

8

NAPOLEON'S GLORIOUS
AFTERLIFE

'Le grand orateur du monde, c'est le succès.'
'The world's great orator is success.'

– Napoleon Bonaparte

'L'homme de génie est un météore destiné à brûler pour
éclairer son siècle.'
'The man of genius is a meteor, destined to burn and enlighten
his century.'

– Napoleon Bonaparte

I

If you are driving along the main east-west highway in the
south of the Czech Republic, and need a toilet stop or a
snack, you might well pull into a service station near the
town of Slavkov u Brna. If you do so, you will probably

park outside a large glass building decorated with the welcoming letters 'WC' and the logo of a famous American hamburger restaurant.

As you leave your car, you will notice that it is being watched over by a moustachioed, rifle-bearing soldier. This is no vigilante security guard – it is a life-size, life-like statue of a Napoleonic infantryman, who seems to be waiting for his colleagues to finish their burgers or come out of the toilets. In fact, the battlefield of Austerlitz is only a few kilometres away, and the statue is mounting a permanent guard over Napoleon's reputation in the region. Every year there is a giant re-enactment of the battle, with Napoleon fans hiking for miles across the countryside to play their part in one of the Emperor's great victories.

Drive closer to the battlefield and Napoleon's presence can be felt even more strongly. Just off the highway is a large cement works. It consists of three tall gantries beside a long conveyor belt that carries raw materials up into the central cement mixer. It would be unremarkable in the industrial landscape were it not for a few decorative details – the three gantries have been wrapped in canvas and painted to resemble Napoleonic artillerymen, while the conveyor belt and factory now look like a giant cannon, mainly thanks to the addition of two painted wheels and a huge bronze-coloured barrel pointing out at the highway. As Napoleonic souvenirs go, it is a gem.

It's hard to imagine any other general inspiring such a gigantic personal monument, especially a foreigner who invaded a country some two centuries earlier. But then

Napoleon has inspired more monuments, both conventional and quirky, than possibly any other historical figure in Europe.

It's a similar story in Warsaw, the Polish capital. In the city's most patriotic location, Warsaw Uprising Square, there stands a bust of Napoleon, in instantly recognisable *petit caporal* hat and waistcoat, above two rampant Napoleonic eagles. It was erected in 2011, on the 190th anniversary of his death, as if the city couldn't wait another ten years for a more meaningful anniversary.

And it is not the only manifestation of Poland's love for the man who annexed the country (sorry – liberated it from Russia, Prussia and Austria) in 1807. Every time the Poles sing the full version of their national anthem, they are reminded of their debt to Napoleon. It is a song of resistance dating back to 1797 and the lyrics, written by Jozef Wybkici, include the lines:

> We shall be Polish,
> Bonaparte has given us the example,
> Of how we should prevail.

Wybkici first sang it to soldiers of the Polish Legion of Napoleon's army, which had been formed with the idea of throwing out their country's Russian, Prussian and Austrian occupiers. Sadly for these valiant patriots, most of them died fighting for Napoleon in Germany, Italy and Haiti, but the French Emperor has obviously been forgiven, and now stands proud in Warsaw, reminding Poles that they were once part of his empire.

Other countries have more surprising homages to history's most famous Frenchman. In 2014, for example, Norway celebrated the 200th anniversary of its constitution – which is based on Napoleonic law – by installing a permanent monument in honour of France in front of Oslo's National Museum of Art. Being Scandinavian, it is less formal than Warsaw's bust of Napoleon: the Norwegian statue consists of three French public toilets, one painted red, one white and one blue, and inscribed 'Liberté', 'Egalité' and 'Fraternité'. Tricolour *toilettes*. But then it is often hard to understand when a Scandinavian is joking.

Even stranger than these toilets, however, is a monument in Belgium, at the site of Waterloo itself, which looks conventional until you realise that it makes you feel as though Napoleon must have won the battle. We have met it already: *Le Panorama de la Bataille de Waterloo*, the 110-metre-long, 12-metre-high picture painted in 1912 by the French artist Louis Dumoulin, who was the official artist to the French navy. The painting was designed to be set inside a round, purpose-built gallery beside the battlefield museum, and depicts the fighting at its fiercest, with cannons blasting, horses charging, and men shouting, shooting and dying. It is a splendidly dramatic picture, and is enhanced by 3D elements like a dummy corpse, discarded weapons and debris-strewn mudbanks, as if it were a huge, gory department store window display.

As mentioned in the introduction to this book, the strangest thing about Dumoulin's work is that it represents a French cavalry charge, and that Wellington, almost hidden in one corner, appears to be on the verge of getting killed. Napoleon, meanwhile, is calmly directing his troops' assault. If a visitor to the building didn't know better, they would assume that the British had been overrun at Waterloo by a horde of snorting Frenchmen. It naturally begs the question why a French artist was invited to paint the grandest memorial on the battlefield. It is as though a German had been asked to decorate a D-Day beach with a panoramic view of machine guns wiping out Allied soldiers as they landed. And it is, of course, proof of the strength of Bonapartist legend, as promulgated by Napoleon's many, and highly influential, admirers.

Right across Europe, Napoleon has left his footprint. Every town in France where he spent any amount of time sells itself to tourists as a *ville impériale*. In Belgium, the Czech Republic, Poland and elsewhere, there are monuments on his battlefields, plaques at inns where he spent the night, 'Napoleon' restaurants where he stopped for a snack, streets and boulevards where his army marched, museums wherever he forgot a pair of socks, even commemorative public toilets in places where he never set foot.

Today, every European knows who the leader of France was in June 1815. Who could say the same about Prussia, Russia, Austria or even England? Bonapartists might accept (grudgingly) that Napoleon lost Waterloo (well, the second half of the battle, anyway), but they can rightly claim that his memory has triumphed. He has been history's winner.

II

The transformation of Napoleon from dead hero to permanent monument began very quickly. In August 1855, when Queen Victoria paid her first state visit to Paris, there was one building she was determined to see. Not the Eiffel Tower, because it wouldn't be built for another thirty-four years; not Notre-Dame, because it was a Catholic church; no, what interested the Anglo-German Queen was a private pilgrimage to Napoleon's tomb. It was dark, there was a terrible thunderstorm brewing, and the torches were spluttering in the wind, but she insisted on going into the gloomy chapel at the Invalides, accompanied by Emperor Napoléon III and several limping old veterans of Napoleon's battles. Not only this, she took her teenaged son, the future King Edward VII, with her, and forced him to kneel before the coffin to pay his respects. All this for the man whom she called in her diary entry for that day 'England's bitterest foe'.

And this was while Napoleon was lying in state in the small Chapelle de Saint-Jérôme, before the completion of the immense mausoleum his nephew Napoléon III was having built below the church. Today, even though Napoleon's tomb doesn't attract the kind of crowds that you see clamouring for a glimpse of the *Mona Lisa* or trying to climb the Eiffel Tower, on a sunny day the gold-encrusted roof of the Invalides dominates the Paris skyline like a torch permanently lit in honour of the former Emperor lying inside.

It is certainly the grandest monument to a dead leader in

the whole Paris region. The body of the Sun King, Louis XIV, was shared out in small portions – his heart donated to the church of Saint Paul in Paris, his entrails to Notre-Dame, the rest of his body to the basilica of Saint-Denis, a suburb that now has an unfortunate reputation for poverty and riotousness, but where French kings were traditionally entombed. Among more than seventy royal tombs dating back to the fifth century, the basilica houses Henri IV, the first of the Bourbons, as well as the fondly remembered François I.

During the Revolution many of the coffins in Saint-Denis were opened and the bodies thrown into mass graves. Most have been reassembled since, but they now seem to huddle together for protection out in the *banlieue*, far from the safety of central Paris where Napoleon reigns supreme in a mausoleum ten times bigger than anything erected for a French king. Even the Chapelle Expiatoire, the memorial built for Louis XVI and Marie-Antoinette by Parisians expressing belated guilt for the double guillotining, is much smaller, and the tragic couple are usually ignored by tourists and Parisians alike.

Visiting Napoleon's tomb, the last word you could possibly imagine is 'loser'. Like the Arc de Triomphe, it is a celebration of victories, though unlike the Arc, which now plays host to an unknown World War One soldier, more recent events don't get a look-in.

The tomb is an underground temple constructed around a brown sarcophagus that looks like a gigantic soft-centred chocolate. The sarcophagus is carved from quartzite, set on a granite plinth, and is guarded by twelve sexy (if somewhat butch) angels who wear off-the-shoulder gowns that reveal large amounts of leg and some hefty cleavage. The angels represent Napoleon's twelve victorious campaigns, though cynical visitors might pick up on the fact that the marble floor is inscribed with only eight victories, including Moscow, which can only be counted as a victory if you ignore the humiliating retreat that followed it.

Around the sarcophagus is a covered walkway decorated with sculpted frescoes. Predictably, one of these contains Napoleon's military record, which was, after all, impressive. He definitely won a lot more battles than he lost (even if you take in the Bonapartist accounting system that divides successful campaigns into several victories and lumps defeats together in a single mass). But, like the inscription on the floor, the record indulges in some dubious barrel-scraping – should the list of victories really include crossing the Saint Bernard's Pass or 'the entry into Madrid'? They sound like stopovers on a coach tour rather than military successes.

Elsewhere, we are confronted by a topless Napoleon (with an enviable six-pack) represented as a Greek god and accompanied by more angels pointing out the extent of his great civil works. An inscription tells us that 'wherever my reign reached, it left lasting traces of its benevolence'. Curiously, these traces include 'la route de Bordeaux', 'le canal de l'Ourcq', and 'les travaux hydrauliques de Dunkerque'. We are also reminded that Napoleon organised a 'five-yearly exhibition of industrial products' and that we have him to thank for the 'renovation of Lyon's factories'. It all reads less like an emperor's boasts than a French engineer's CV.

There is another panel dedicated to Napoleon's *cour des comptes* (national auditors' administration), on which we see the guardian angel of accountancy watching over receipts and outgoings, as well as one given over to Napoleon's introduction of *centralisation administrative*. In short, the tomb seems to be telling us that if heaven needs a techno-crat with excellent organisational skills, Napoleon is the man for the job.

It is true that many – if not most – of the people visiting the Invalides are going there principally to see the army museum rather than the tomb, but then Napoleon is the star of that too. And after all, what foreign visitor would dream of visiting France's army museum for anything other than Napoleon's *Grande Armée*? There hasn't been much to shout about since.

The museum doesn't disappoint – if, that is, the visitor is fascinated by the legend of the Napoleonic soldier. There are rooms full of their glossy weapons – richly engraved swords, muskets made of polished wood and topped by the famously intimidating bayonets – as well as the campaign uniforms of many of Napoleon's regiments. It is a parade rather than a battlefield.

The museum frankly admits that Napoleon was a war-maker, but doesn't seem to disapprove. 'Combining revolutionary ideas and his own glory,' one inscription reads, 'Napoleon created a great empire that remodelled the face of Europe.' (Non-Bonapartists might interpret this 'remodelling' as breaking Europe's nose and smothering its mouth in French lipstick.) 'The enemies of France were neutralised,' another caption tells us, an aggressive boast that it is rare to find in a modern military museum. Most countries now play down their former attempts at 'neutralising' other nations.

Napoleon's ultimate defeat is acknowledged in the tiny Waterloo Room, which is maybe 10 feet square. Here, for once, the museum recognises the existence of Napoleon's opponents, who are represented by three English swords and a frilly black Hussar's jacket that looks like something out of a Parisian madame's boudoir, a stark contrast to the manliness of the *Grande Armée's* uniforms – a subliminal suggestion, perhaps, that these effete Englishmen really didn't deserve to win at Waterloo (if, indeed, they won at all).

An electronic display describes the course of the battle in five minutes, while the audioguide toes the Bonapartist line, telling us that everything was going more or less to plan when the Prussians arrived and 'upset the course of the battle', as if its true course ought to have been a French victory. An inscription on the wall sums up the outcome of Waterloo as 'an accumulation of bad luck, errors and communication problems'. At least they don't blame the weather.

The film on this electronic display is very restrained, with little arrows to indicate the movement of the different armies, tiny electronic puffs of smoke to simulate cannon fire, and bangs and neighing horse effects to add a little atmosphere.

The only sign that the battle might have involved anything

more violent than neighing and puffs of smoke is a breastplate with a large cannonball-shaped hole in the front. A
certain Carabinier Antoine Fauveau was one Napoleonic
soldier who never made it back to France.

The Napoleon section of the national army museum is less
a commemoration of the men who gave their lives for their
Emperor than a celebration of Napoleon's sense of style
and grandeur. Even while he was alive, he turned himself
and his entourage into monuments.

Napoleon's sense of style is, of course, one of the reasons
why he remains so firmly fixed in modern minds. He created
a personal look that is as unmistakeable as Marilyn Monroe's
blond curls or the skinny silhouette of Michael Jackson.

The green jacket and tight white trousers (the uniform
of a *chasseur*, a light cavalryman); the grey greatcoat and
white waistcoat that he showed to royalist troops in March
1815, defying them to shoot at their instantly recognisable
Emperor; and of course the black bicorn hat. With these
simple elements, Napoleon created the mould for all military
dictators since – design yourself a personal uniform so that
the people will think of you as an active soldier, no matter
how flabby and battle-shy you really get (not that Napoleon
became either before he was deposed).

Napoleon wanted to distance himself from the silk-and-
satin rulers who had preceded him, as well as impose a
forceful new image of military power, with himself as the
charismatic protector of the nation. In reality, he often
fought battles wearing a green velvet cap or bareheaded (as

he was at Waterloo), but he created his iconic image as early as 1801, when the painter Jean-Baptiste Isabey first sketched him in green jacket and black hat, with his hand inside his waistcoat – not because of stomach pain or to hide a paunch but because this was seen at the time as a noble orator's stance.

During his fifteen-year on-and-off reign as consul and Emperor, Napoleon had about fifty of the bicorn hats made out of felt or beaver skin by a Parisian hatter in the Palais Royal, and from 1801 onwards all his official portraits depicted him wearing it – the only exceptions being the pictures painted for his two coronations. In 1806, for example, two years after his enthronement as Emperor, he commissioned a portrait from Europe's most fashionable painter, Ingres, for which he posed in a Roman emperor's crown of golden laurel leaves, wearing a jewelled broadsword and sporting a manly (and physiologically inaccurate) cleft chin – all in all, every bit as godlike as France's most elitist kings. But this, and the even more pompous painting of his second coronation, are rare departures from the brand image that his soldiers loved and (while their glory lasted) his people idolised.

This sense of design extended throughout his regime, which was characterised by its mass of new uniforms and its ever-present golden eagles. Napoleon even seems to have invented the ministerial red box – all generals and ranking administrators in Bonapartist France had their own official document case, which was often red, and inscribed with their title.

The Napoleonic look found favour outside France, too:

after all, ever since the Battle of Waterloo, Britain's Household Cavalry and Guards regiments have worn the French breast-plates, busbies and eagles that they picked up from the battlefield. One could interpret this as a kind of scalping, decorating yourself with symbols of your defeated opponents. But surely it is more of a testimony to the attractive design – we have never seen British or American troops sporting swastikas or jackboots (except perhaps when a British soldier-prince goes to a fancy dress party).

And talking of Nazis, it has to be said again: in matters of design Napoleon seems – inadvertently of course – to have inspired Hitler. All those eagles, the personalised uniforms of the Third Reich's leaders, the highly choreo-graphed processions of adoring soldiers, the charismatic portraits. Even Hitler's floppy black fringe – it's all Napoleon. And it's the only historical tribute the modern Bonapartist would prefer to do without.

III

Aside from grand monuments like Invalides and the Arc de Triomphe, Napoleon and his short reign have left a mark on everyday life in modern France in a way that no other period of history has done.

There is, for instance, an Avenue Charles de Gaulle and a Place 8 Mai 1945 in many a French town, but the sheer multitude of Napoleonic streets in Paris is dizzying. The city is ringed by the *boulevards des maréchaux*, just inside the modern *périphérique*, as if Napoleon's men were now defending Paris against attack from the notoriously unruly *banlieusards*. Out of his twenty-six marshals, nineteen of them have a boulevard named after them, the most notable exceptions being Grouchy, who went AWOL at Waterloo, and the traitors Marmont (who defected to the royalists in 1814) and Bernadotte (who, bizarrely, left Napoleon's army to become King of Sweden in 1810, and later signed an alliance with Russia agaist France). Even Ney, whose rashness and indecision scuppered Napoleon's battle plan at Waterloo, gets a boulevard.*

Throughout Paris there are countless other testimonies to Napoleon – the rue Bonaparte, leading from Saint Germain des Prés to the River Seine; streets like Friedland, Iéna (Jena), Pyramides, Wagram, Marengo and Rivoli named after his victories, a couple of which get bridges too (Iéna and Austerlitz), and one a railway station: Austerlitz is the anti-Russian and anti-Austrian equivalent of London's Francophobic Waterloo.

There is nothing forcing the French to maintain these nostalgic names. After the Revolution, for example, most royal street names were expunged, but no such fate has befallen Napoleon.

The only exception was the rue Napoléon itself, a grand

---

* These, by the way, were not named by Napoleon himself, or as part of his nephew Napoléon III's later campaign to glorify the family's image – they were created in the 1920s, just after the slaughter in the trenches, when France decided to look to the more distant past to boost its patriotic image. This was also when the French adopted Joan of Arc as their patron saint. Napoleon and Joan – the twin saviours of the nation.

street in central Paris that he commissioned in his own honour in 1806, to replace a demolished convent – proof that in Napoleon's world view, emperors took preference over divinities. The street led to the Place Vendôme, where Napoleon erected a column in honour of the *Grande Armée*, made from 1,200 bronze cannons captured at Austerlitz. As soon as Napoleon abdicated in 1814, the street was renamed rue de la Paix – Peace Street – the obvious implication being that Napoleon's name was synonymous with war.

His column in the Place Vendôme survived the invasion by British, Austrian and Russian troops, but was pulled down in 1871 by the Communards (Parisians who resisted the Prussian siege of 1870–1 and then staged a short-lived revolution), who called it a 'symbol of brute force and false glory, an affirmation of militarism, a negation of international law, a permanent insult by victors to the defeated' – probably the strongest-ever condemnation of Napoleon's rule by the French themselves. However, the Commune lasted only a few months, and as soon as it fell, the column went up again, even though the new government was theoretically a republican regime. Even today, 42 metres above one of Paris's most luxurious squares, Napoleon in his Roman toga looks down on his old capital, apparently keeping his eye out for dubious goings-on at the Ritz Hotel.

The column even survived World War Two, when the hotel was squatted by the Luftwaffe and adopted as the epicentre of Nazi nightlife. The occupiers clearly didn't object to being lorded over by Napoleon. Here was one Frenchman whom even these descendants of the warlike Prussians could respect.

IV

Napoleon's legacy in everyday France is not confined to road names and military mementoes. Far from it.

It was during his reign that European streets first got their present numbering system, with even numbers on one side, odd on the other. It was also his engineers who designated that pavements should be slightly convex, with gutters collecting the run-off (although efficient sewers were still decades in the future and much of the run-off would have made disgusting stains on the Emperor's shiny boots).

Napoleon, who as we saw above was the French god of centralisation, also decided that Paris should have one big central market at Les Halles, and that the city needed large abattoirs on the outskirts, so that butchers would stop cutting animals' throats in their shops and courtyards and offending sensitive Parisians.

Napoleon also decreed that Parisians needed to be centralised after death, and created the large cemeteries of Père Lachaise, Montparnasse and Montmartre.

Modern tourists have plenty of reasons to be grateful to Napoleon, too, even if they don't want to visit his tomb, or be entombed themselves alongside Oscar Wilde and Jim Morrison in Père Lachaise. Because the Louvre owes much of its collection to *l'Empereur* and his empire-building instincts.

A national art collection had been started in 1793, largely consisting of works that had been 'liberated' from the Church or the royal family during the Revolution. Napoleon began to contribute to the collection as soon as he was named chief of the French army based in Italy in 1796. All French generals were under orders to 'send to France all the artistic and scientific monuments that they consider worthy of entering our museums and libraries', and Napoleon fulfilled his mission with the same thoroughness he applied to any task, pillaging Europe's art collections – including that of the Vatican – of its finest pictures, sculptures and manuscripts. In 1800, on seizing power, he moved the collection to the Louvre, ironically evicting a large group of artists who had been squatting there since the Revolution. He also decided that the country's art collection needed to be centralised, and dispossessed many provincial museums of their prize exhibits.

Inevitably, after he lost power in 1815, the occupiers returned the compliment and tried to relieve France of its stolen property. By November of that year, five months after Waterloo, 5,203 works of art, including 2,065 paintings, among them several dozen Rembrandts, seventy-five Rubens, fifteen Raphaels, as well as Da Vincis,* Van Dycks and Titians, and hundreds of ancient Roman and Greek statues, had been sent back to their previous owners.

The Pope commissioned an artist, Antonio Canova, to retrieve works that had been looted from the Vatican, no doubt on the grounds that Canova knew Napoleon's collections well – he had previously made a sculpture of Napoleon

---

* The *Mona Lisa* wasn't one of them because it had been bought legally by King François I soon after Da Vinci's death in 1519.

as a giant Greek athlete, naked except for a fig leaf, which was later bought by Wellington and displayed in his London town house, in the same way that a big-game hunter might have shown off the skin of a tiger he had shot.* Seeing these foreigners loot the Louvre's (largely looted) collection, the museum's director, Dominique Vivant Denon, who had accompanied Napoleon to Egypt to requisition ancient arte-facts, complained to King Louis XVIII that 'We conquered Europe to construct this trophy; Europe has now joined forces to destroy it.'

Fortunately for modern visitors to Paris, Monsieur Denon was over-dramatising somewhat. Because even while Wellington was (so French historians allege) personally climbing ladders to unhook paintings from the walls of the museum, the Parisians were hiding large quantities of stolen art from the prying eyes of the invaders. At the same time, in typical Parisian fashion, the Louvre informed provincial museums that they wouldn't be getting their exhibits back. Which is why today, visitors to Paris can still enjoy the cream of France's art collection – as well as a large number of pieces that were never returned to other countries – all under one roof. *Vive la centralisation napoléonienne*.

---

* The statue of the naked Napoleon is still on show at Apsley House, at Hyde Park Corner, alongside an impressive selection of artworks given to Wellington by the Spanish as thanks for chasing out its French invaders. Significantly, the English Heritage website declares that 'pride of place' in the whole collection goes to Napoleon.

V

After 1815, Napoleon's family was banned *en masse* from France. This enraged one of his greatest fans, the writer Victor Hugo, who turned his most withering irony on Louis XVIII's administration. What had the Bonapartes done wrong? Hugo asked, and ironised: 'Here are their crimes – religion restored, the Civil Code written, France expanded beyond its natural borders, Marengo, Iéna, Wagram, Austerlitz; it is the greatest legacy of power and glory that any great man ever gave to a great nation.'

Napoleon himself, never one to undervalue his contribution to France's well-being, told his biographer Las Cases much the same thing. He had bequeathed to the nation, he said, 'the glory and splendour . . . of truly national institutions'. Only a true French technocrat could ever think that a country's bureaucracies were glorious and splendid, and far from being the belligerent little Corsican that many British people imagine, Napoleon was in fact a passionate administrator obsessed with every detail of political and public life, from the titles of his ministers to the colour of his soldiers' trousers.

Even his fiercest critics would have to admit that modern France is a Napoleonic nation.

French law today is still founded upon the Code Napoléon of 1804 (later renamed the Code Civil), which set out all the rights and responsibilities of a French citizen. It was followed by the Code du Commerce of 1807 (designed to promote 'free commerce that favours all classes and excites all imaginations') and the Code Pénal of 1810, which among other things created the very French *juge d'instruction*, the examining magistrate who even today conducts criminal investigations, interrogating suspects and witnesses, over-riding the police whenever he or she feels like it, and often taking years to decide whether a case should come to court.

However, these laws weren't merely the whims of a dictator. Napoleon summoned four legal specialists from different regions of France, aiming to combine the best elements of all the country's 360 regional legal systems. Each of the specialists' proposals was examined by teams of advisers, and then voted on by an assembly. For a man renowned as a tyrant, it was as democratic as anything France had ever seen, including during the Revolution.

The laws themselves generally favoured individual freedom. Any ordinary citizen could own property, a ruling that ended the semi-feudal system still reigning in the French countryside. The only excuse for withdrawing this inalienable right to property was *l'utilité publique*, which today explains how French railways and motorways get built so fast – a Frenchman's home is no longer his *château* if the state decides to demolish it 'for the public good'.

The Code Napoléon also established the very French concept of the *co-propriété*, a group of individuals who own apartments in the same building. The system is still very much alive today, which is why anyone who owns an apart-ment in France is summoned every year by registered letter to attend a *co-propriété* meeting, chaired by an elected pres-ident, at which everyone spends hours debating what colour to paint front doors within the building (they all have to be the same colour), who is responsible for repairing which walls, and how much money to set aside for the following year's expenses, as if preparing for a Napoleonic campaign. Two people even have to be conscripted Napoleon-style to serve as the president and secretary of the *co-propriété*.

The Code Napoléon also made marriage a state rather than a religious institution, freeing it from moralistic overtones, and declared everyone free to work without belonging to a guild – a right that France's trade unions have been trying to undo ever since. In short, Napoleon was trying to give each of his citizens – including those throughout his European empire – the right to control their own lives.

Not that he believed in equal rights. This was democracy drafted by men for men. In the Code Napoléon, women were described as 'minors', incapable of managing their own affairs. A wife could only work if she had her husband's permission, and her wages would be paid to him. Women were not allowed to vote or sign contracts, and apparently did not need education beyond primary school. They were free to be prostitutes and sleep with married men, whose wives couldn't sue for divorce unless the man actually invited his other sexual partner to live in the family home. Just sleeping around was no grounds for divorce – unless you were a woman, of course: your husband could get rid of you for the slightest infidelity.

Most of this sexism has been taken out of the Code since then, though some of its more obscure clauses are still being modernised today. In fifteen places, the text of laws still in force in France in early 2014 referred to a citizen's obligation to manage life 'like a good family father', a phrase borrowed from the *pater familias* in ancient Roman law. Only now have these been changed to read 'in a reasonable way'. But then France has always been slightly slow in giving equal rights to women – universal suffrage for twenty-one-year-old female voters was not granted until 1945.

Overall, though, Napoleon's laws have such universal appeal that they form the basis of the legal systems in modern Belgium, Quebec, Mauritius, Senegal, the Netherlands, Italy, Spain, former French colonies in North Africa, some Latin American republics, and the American state of Louisiana (which was a French possession until Napoleon sold it in 1803).

As Napoleon himself said: 'My true glory is not to have won forty battles; Waterloo will erase the memory of so many victories. That which nothing will erase, and that will live forever, is my Code Civil.'

He wasn't wrong. Except that, in the eyes of his French fans, Waterloo has erased none of his glory either.

VI

It is a huge cliché to call any dictatorial Frenchman a Napoleon, especially if he is below average height; but like many clichés, it is based on truth. Whatever their height, all modern French presidents are fairly Napoleonic in their annoyance at being forced to dilute their power by working with a prime minister and a parliament. Nicolas Sarkozy famously ignored his and ruled alone. And whoever the president, the role of *premier ministre* is a fragile one. He (it is virtually always a he) can be replaced at the drop of a hat (or a drop in the polls) by the autocratic president, who, of course, lives and works in Napoleon's old palace, l'Elysée, amid an imperial decor of gilded chairs and chandeliers, waited upon by servants and surrounded by a court of Napoleonic technocrats. In effect, *l'Empereur* is still in power.

And if Napoleon were to rise from his sarcophagus – and no doubt win the next presidential election by a landslide given the current state of French politics – he would also get a glow of satisfaction when touring the country and giving his young citizens a pinch on the cheek (one of his favourite occupations while he was alive).

Because France's education system is almost exactly as he outlined it more than two centuries ago. Admittedly, French children can now learn things that didn't exist at the time, like computer science and rugby; and – shock, horror – girls are allowed to attend educational establishments for just as long as boys. But the structure of the system is entirely Napoleonic.

In 1806, after drafting his bill of citizens' rights, Napoleon set about reforming education, declaring that he wanted 'the son of a farmer to be able to say: one day I will be a cardinal, a marshal or a minister'. Even given the fact that he obviously preferred farmers' *daughters* to have no ambitions higher than becoming a farmer's wife, it was a strong statement of social mobility that was true to the purest principles of the Revolution.

His new system included the primary school, the *collège* (for the first four years of secondary education), the *lycée* (for the final three years), and a range of university-like schools that still exist today.

Napoleon had already founded *lycées* in 1802, saying that they were designed 'to educate the elite of the nation' (that is to say, boys), and he had centralised matters so that the same lessons were given at the same time in each *lycée* in the country. The head of each *lycée* was, as he or she is today, an imperiously aloof, non-teaching administrator called a *proviseur*. The only real change to the *lycée* regime is that nowadays, the beginning and end of each lesson is no longer marked by a military drum roll, a system that lasted for more than 100 years.

Napoleon also created the diploma that most French children aim for at the end of their secondary education – the *baccalauréat*, a name taken from *baccalaureus*, the medieval French for a young man training to become either a scholar or a knight.* Napoleon divided the qualification into two parts – the *baccalauréat de lettres* and the *baccalauréat de sciences*, a basic division that still exists in the twenty-first century.

In 1808, there were only twenty-one candidates – all male, of course. And things took a long time to change. The first woman who was actually allowed to take the *baccalauréat* was Julie-Victoire Daublé, who passed the exam in 1861. It wasn't until 1924 that all girls were allowed to study as far as the *baccalauréat* as a matter of course.

---

* The Middle Ages was apparently the time when French males first decided to divide themselves into two distinct groups: intellectuals and men of action.

It wasn't only the *lycée* that was meant to turn out an educated French elite. Napoleon also founded further education schools designed to forge a nation of technocrats.

The Ecole Polytechnique, for example, already existed as a science academy when he decided in 1804 to give it military status and a new motto: 'Pour la Patrie, les Sciences et la Gloire' ('For the Nation, Sciences and Glory'). In 1814, its uniformed students earned their epaulettes by mounting barricades in the east of Paris against the advancing Prussians. They still have to do army service today, and can regularly be seen on 14 July, a herd of nerds marching awkwardly down the Champs-Elysées in their Napoleonic uniforms, their swords swinging by their sides in case any Prussians decide to disrupt the Bastille Day celebrations.

It is a similar story for the Ecole Normale Supérieure, still France's top teacher-training academy. Now, as in Napoleon's day, the school turns out 100 graduates per year, all of whom are selected via a hellishly difficult entrance exam that requires two years of cramming after the *baccalauréat*. The ENS was originally set up in 1795, then abandoned. Napoleon revived the idea in 1808, adapting it to be more rigid and military. The system was considered so Napoleonic that the school was shut down by the royalists in 1822, only to be reopened in 1826, presumably because pupils were getting out of hand and needed Napoleonic discipline.

Bad discipline in class is a danger that modern France does not want to face. Not all of its teachers go through the ENS – many are recruited from university – but most French kids would testify that they are taught in a style that owes plenty to *l'Empereur*. If he sat in on lessons in almost any French school today, from primary up to the second or third year of tertiary education, he would almost certainly recognise his teaching method – the notion that I, the marshal/educator, am here to order you, the humble squaddie/pupil, to learn the universally recognised truth. So shut up and listen. Just as in an army, the lower ranks (the students) in the French education system are not encouraged to have opinions – after all, battles are lost if subordinates start questioning orders. Waterloo was lost (well, only partially won, anyway) because a few foot-soldiers decided, in spite of the assurances of their officers, that the *Garde* were retreating and that it wasn't wise to hang around. Opinions and other signs of unruliness there-fore have to be banned at the very least until the third or fourth year of university, at which point a committee of marshals (or professors) will decide whether they are valid or not.

What it boils down to – and French schoolchildren can confirm this – is that students are lined up like Napoleon's infantry and have knowledge fired at them as if from a cannon. If some fall, it doesn't matter, because enough will be left standing until the *baccalauréat* or beyond to ensure that the nation as a whole is educated and survives. It's brutal, but it's efficient.

Napoleon would be proud to see his system in action today, turning out French minds that are as rigidly trained

as those of the men he used to send walking unquestion-
ingly towards the opposing side's artillery.

VII

Napoleon's image as the founder of the modern French
nation is so strongly defended by his admirers that he also
gets credit for plenty of things he didn't do.

It is often alleged that he invented France's favourite loaf,
the baguette. This is an historic falsehood that even gets
repeated on the websites of French flour companies, keen
to sell their patriotic products.

The most common version of the story is that Napoleon
wanted a straight loaf that his soldiers could carry in a
pocket in their trousers. No one seems to question why
anyone would actually want to stick a bread stick down their
trousers, but it is a legend that is often repeated.

In fact, of course, it would be absurd to give a man on
the march the kind of bread that goes stale after about three
hours, and starts to disintegrate within a day. No soldier
wanted to march across the Russian steppes with his
breeches full of breadcrumbs. What Napoleon's troops
needed was a thick-crusted, moist loaf that would stay fresh
for days: definitely not a baguette.

As I pointed out in my book *1000 Years of Annoying the
French*, the baguette was introduced into France by one of
Napoleon's conquerors, Austria, where, in the mid-nineteenth
century, an oven was developed that could produce bread
with a thin crust, a light, fluffy dough and a short shelf life.

A tough campaigning general like Napoleon would never have approved of anything so frivolous and impractical – except, perhaps, for his own table.

It is also often said that Napoleon got his scientists to invent the process of turning beetroot into sugar. The (highly credible) argument is that, faced with a British blockade of his ports and a self-imposed ban on importing British sugar – his Blocus Continental – Napoleon looked to home-grown solutions for sweetening his coffee and crème brûlée.*

In fact, the extraction of sugar from vegetables dates back to 1747, when the process was developed by a German scientist called Andreas Sigismund Marggraf. One of his students, a man called Franz Karl Achard, began selectively breeding sugar beets, and opened a sugar refinery in 1801, sponsored by one of Napoleon's enemies, Friedrich Wilhelm III of Prussia. When the Blocus Continental took effect, and sugar supplies were further depleted by a revolt of France's slaves in Haiti, Napoleon offered a one million franc grant for the development of sugar-beet technology in France, and in 1812 issued a decree ordering farmers to plant beets, a dictatorial move that has earned him an unwarranted place in the heart of every Frenchman with a sweet tooth.

It was a case of wartime necessity accelerating existing technology – a much less destructive equivalent of World War Two pushing nuclear scientists to make atom bombs. (Although dentists might not agree.)

---

* By the way, crème brûlée isn't entirely French, either – it's a seventeenth-century adaptation of the ancient Arabian recipe for crème caramel.

We can be sure that if Napoleon really had invented the baguette and sugar beet, he would have dictated a chapter about it to Las Cases, and his underground tomb in Paris would include a fresco of a semi-naked Bonaparte spreading jam on to a long slice of French bread, surrounded on one side by an angel caressing a pair of sugar beets, and on the other by an infantryman with a baguette protruding from his trousers.

VIII

Today there are plenty of occasions when it is still possible to hear French shouts of 'Vive l'Empereur!'

First there are the auctions of Napoleonic memorabilia, which always attract crowds and generate high prices. I have met surviving members of the Bonaparte family (of which there are many, because anyone with a milligram of Napoleonic DNA is very keen for it to be known) who admitted that 'every time we need some money to refurbish the chateau, we take a sword down off the wall'. And just one sword could pay for quite a few rolls of wallpaper – in 2007, the sabre that Napoleon carried at the Battle of Marengo in 1800 sold for 4.8 million euros.

In March 2008, when former French Prime Minister (and Bonapartist historian) Dominique de Villepin sold his collection of Napoleonic books and documents, huge prices were paid for anything that had belonged to the Emperor himself. An autograph went for 28,000 euros, and when a French museum snapped up a British anti-Bonaparte pamphlet, spectators shouted 'Vive l'Empereur!' A battle against *les Anglais* had been won.

In November 2013, a mere copy of Napoleon's will – a document that had not been signed by the Emperor himself – created huge excitement when it came up for public auction at the Drouot salesroom (Paris's biggest auction house, coincidentally named after the Napoleonic marshal). Several TV news crews came along to witness the great historical event. As the auction began, a man moved through the crowd whispering 'I am the Emperor reborn'. Sadly, no one believed him.

Before the will itself came up, bidding for lesser Napoleonic items was brisk. An engraving of a battle got two men at the back of the room arguing about whether it was a victory or not – 'a victory, surely, most of them were', they concluded. When the will – or, let's not forget, an anonymous copy of it – was announced, the cameras clicked on, and necks began swivelling to see who was bidding. The numbers rose rapidly, spurred on by telephone and internet bids, until a Frenchman in the room clinched the deal for an amazing 180,000 euros. His only comment as he left the room was that he was 'bidding on behalf of a collector'.

In November 2014, a huge sale of Napoleonic memora- bilia was held in Fontainebleau, the self-declared 'imperial town' just south of Paris. Admittedly the auction was happening for a less-than-flattering reason – Prince Albert of Monaco was emptying his Musée des Souvenirs Napoléoniens to make way for a museum dedicated to his mother, Princess Grace – but that didn't bother the Napoleonic collectors because it meant that hundreds of rare items were coming up for grabs. There was such a frenzy of bidding that almost every lot at least doubled its estimate, with some going ten times over the expected price. Pairs of stockings actually worn by Napoleon sold for more than 15,000 euros. Clippings of his hair fetched the same price, and one of the black bicorn hats that Napoleon wore himself, and then gifted to his vet, went for a dizzying 1.8 million euros.

As the hat came up for sale, the auctioneer quoted a few lines of poetry written in its honour by Edmond Rostand in his play *L'Aiglon* ('the eagle chick' was the nickname of Napoleon's son, also called Napoleon), first performed in 1900. The lines describing the Emperor's trademark head-gear can be loosely translated as follows:

Large black seashell that the waves have brought,
And in which one's ear, when held close, hears
The wave of sound that a great nation makes as it marches.

The warm round of applause the auctioneer received for his poem said a lot more about French nostalgia than his reciting skills. He got the second and third lines completely wrong, but no one cared: in everyone's minds, just for this day France was on the march again, rather than being bogged down in post–credit-crunch austerity. And all thanks to Napoleon.

The last two bidders in the race for the hat after the price broke the million barrier were a Chinese woman and a Korean man. When the Korean won,* there was more applause. No one seemed particularly worried that this important Napoleonic artefact would be leaving France – for a start, there are several of his hats in French museums and private collections; but perhaps most importantly, Bonapartists probably saw the outrageous price as satisfying proof that Napoleon's star is starting to shine far beyond the borders of France and his European empire.

But perhaps the most notable thing about all these sales was that the auctioneers referred to Napoleon throughout as 'l'Empereur'. Each time, for a few hours, he was back on his throne.

Several times a year, in France and throughout his former empire, Napoleon really does return. Whenever there is a battle re-enactment, the cries of 'Vive l'Empereur!' are almost as loud as the barrages of blank-firing artillery. And Napoleon himself is always there to acknowledge them.

Every period of military history has its re-enactors – at the 2014 commemoration of the seventieth anniversary of D-Day there were even uniformed Nazis (though it is to be hoped that they don't re-enact all the Nazis' exploits). Napoleonic battles are probably the most frequently commemorated in Europe, and attract large numbers of enthusiasts from all

---

* He was bidding on behalf of a Korean poultry company that wanted to display the hat, a sword and other items acquired at the sale in its Seoul head office, to prove to its staff and customers that the company was, like Napoleon, a winner. News of Waterloo, it seems, never reached Korea.

sides, no doubt because the uniforms are so brightly coloured and the formations of lines and squares so aesthetically pleasing. A Napoleonic battle was a grand, highly choreographed affair, unlike, say, a re-enactment of Passchendaele that would involve little more than waves of men in dirt-coloured uniforms tumbling face-first into mud.

The difference between the re-enactors in Napoleon's armies and the others seems to be that some of them are not pretending.

In 2014 I witnessed this at first hand at Brienne le Château, the site of the battle – a skirmish, really – that took place in January 1814, when Napoleon was fighting his last-ditch stand against the invading Prussians. Two hundred years later, the town decided to celebrate the Emperor's victory – in May, so that re-enactment soldiers would not get too cold or wet – and to follow the fighting with a huge public picnic rather than the looting of corpses and the crude amputation of shattered limbs.

At the re-enactment, about 400 or so French cavalry and infantry, all dressed in authentic uniforms and carrying realistic weapons, charged about twenty valiant Prussians who were 'holding the castle' (or more accurately, occupying part of the lawn).

The line of French infantry advanced, stopping periodically to fire their muskets, and occasionally getting a bit over-enthusiastic. One volley (of blanks, naturally) was aimed straight at the French spectators, who were turned into accidental Prussians. Another group of footsoldiers fired as their own horsemen were riding past, forcing the announcer to admit that 'the French infantry shooting at the French cavalry is a bit embarrassing'.

But the mass of Napoleonic troops so outnumbered the enemy that they could afford a few casualties from friendly fire, and after no more than fifteen minutes, the lines of French infantry had walked right up to the Prussians, provoking a brief waving of bayonets, a rapid retreat of the invaders, and a rapturous cry from the announcer that 'The allies have been routed! Victory has been won!'

The only problem was that the French artillery didn't seem to agree. The battle had been so short they had only had time to fire one or two salvoes, so even as a very convincing Napoleon imitator was congratulating his victorious troops, his cannons kept up a ceaseless barrage of deafening explosions.

At first, the announcer politely asked for a ceasefire – 'Arrêtez, s'il vous plaît!' – but when they carried on regardless, he lost his temper, yelling, 'L'artillerie, stop!' Yes, an English word aimed at French artillerymen. No wonder they ignored him, and one cannon, luckily firing nothing more dangerous than shreds of newspaper, almost blew Napoleon's head off as he was walking towards them to impose some discipline. At which point the announcer, dressed as a nineteenth-century gentleman, strutted over and confiscated the artillerymen's plungers. A tactic that proved so effective that it's a wonder Wellington didn't try it sooner at Waterloo.

Overall, though, morale in the French camp was high. The Napoleon imitator, his safety now assured, toured the battlefield, instantly recognisable in his bicorn hat and grey overcoat, congratulating each unit in turn. His troops saluted him, waving their busbies and helmets in the air, just like the good old days, while the announcer informed the crowd that 'if we still had the French empire, we could have saved all the lives lost during the First World War. Vive l'Empereur!'

Reassuringly, perhaps, most of the spectators were stunned into silence by this radical rewriting of history, and only the soldiers took up the cry. But it is hard to imagine similar speeches being made at other re-enactments. Would a man in Viking costume bemoan the fact that Scandinavians are no longer allowed to pillage England? Does someone dressed as Wellington tell his modern redcoats: 'If we still had George III, we could all wear white wigs and talk to trees without anyone laughing at us'? No, and surely only the more fanatical of the Napoleonic re-enactors really wish that the past would return.

After the battle, I talked to some of the troops, and asked a footsoldier why he didn't get himself an officer's uniform so that he could wave his sword about, give orders, and maybe even have a drink with the Napoleon impersonator. (Only a select few plumed officers were allowed to sit down with *l'Empereur* himself outside his fenced-off imperial bivouac.) Oh no, I was told, that wouldn't go down well. You can't just decide to be an officer in the official Napoleonic re-enactment groups. And besides, it costs a fortune to be an officer – an authentic, hand-made uniform (the only ones permitted) would cost more than 10,000 euros. Even an ordinary infantryman's shoulder straps cost

100 euros from the official suppliers. This is a cause that requires true devotion.

At the time of writing, fresh epaulettes and shoulder straps are no doubt being stitched and starched for the 200th anniversary re-enactment of Waterloo. And guess who is depicted on the home page of the official 'Waterloo 2015' website, and who is the most visible figure on the official poster, about five times bigger than his two rivals. Wellington? Blücher? No, Napoleon – or rather a Napoleon imitator, the reincarnation of the Emperor. Bonaparte is back. The modern-day Bonapartists have taken possession of the battlefield.

Apparently, in June 2015 over 5,000 uniformed enthusiasts will be replaying the Battle of Waterloo, which will be spread over two days instead of trying to cram all the action into one, as the original combatants had to do. And this time, you can bet the French will be going for a victory.

In some ways, of course, they have already won that victory. As we have seen, Napoleon is already the biggest star of the battlefield museum. His is the name, and the silhouette, that everyone recognises from that period of history. His shadow looms over modern French institutions and those he set up all over Europe. He is also the general whose tomb dominates his former capital city's skyline, and whose naked statue holds pride of place in Wellington's former home in London. And now he is even conquering Asia.

9

FRANCE WON WATERLOO, EVEN IF NAPOLEON DIDN'T

'Napoléon a laissé la France écrasée, envahie, vidée de sang et de courage, plus petite qu'il ne l'avait prise.'
'Napoleon left France crushed, invaded, drained of blood and courage, smaller than when he took it.'

– Charles de Gaulle in his book
La France et son armée (1938)

'Le bonheur de la France dépendait de la perte de la bataille.'
'France's happiness depended on losing the battle.'

– nineteenth-century French publisher (and royalist)
Jean-Gabriel Dentu

I

When Napoleon was shipped off to Saint Helena, the returning Louis XVIII and his entourage weren't the only people in France who thought that the South Atlantic wasn't far enough. The same goes today. There are plenty of French people who despise everything that Napoleon stood for – his despotism, the number of lives he threw away in battle, the way he has inspired every foreigner to giggle at any authoritative Frenchman.

These people willingly accept that Napoleon was beaten in Belgium on 18 June 1815. But this doesn't necessarily mean that they think France lost the battle. For them, getting rid of Bonaparte simply gave the country the breathing space to become the great nation that it is today. They view Waterloo as a victory for France itself. To them, the British and the Prussians were almost unimportant by-standers in France's great leap forward.

Before Waterloo, there were already voices complaining about Napoleon's reign, though they had to tread carefully for fear of reprisals. In December 1813, Joseph Lainé, the MP for the Gironde in south-western France, made a daring speech in parliament complaining that 'trade has been destroyed, and industry is dying. What are the causes of this unspeakable misery? A vexatious administration, excessive taxation . . . and crueller still, the way our armies are recruited.' Lainé represented the Bordeaux region, which was suffering more than most from Napoleon's *droits réunis*, a VAT-style duty on everyday goods to raise money for his warmongering. Wine was taxed at a staggering 94.1 per cent. Not only that, Napoleon had forbidden the region's ports from selling wine to their traditional buyers, the thirsty Brits.

This was why, when Wellington chased Napoleon's army across the Spanish border and invaded southern France in 1814, Bordeaux greeted him as a liberator. At the same time, French royalists began campaigning in the area, promising 'an end to tyranny, war, conscription and *droits réunis*'. It was a message that many wanted to hear.

When talking about Napoleon's first abdication in 1814, Bonapartist historians often fail to mention that he only just made it alive to the south coast of France because of the hostility of his own people. Even Walter Scott's account of French people 'insulting his passage' doesn't paint the full picture. As Napoleon's convoy of carriages passed through Orgon, in Provence, there was a minor riot, and he had to disguise himself as a messenger to save his skin. He also insisted on taking a British warship across to Elba, because the French navy was under the command of his rival, the treacherous Talleyrand, and Napoleon suspected that he might 'fall overboard' during the crossing. The French sailors designated to escort the Emperor were sent away at the last minute, and Napoleon entrusted himself to the hated – but apparently more honourable – British enemy.

Today, even some of the French historians who admire Napoleon, like Jean Tulard, author of *Le Dictionnaire Napoléon*, acknowledge the dictatorial tendencies that created such hostility while the Emperor was still in power. Tulard quotes the story of Cincinnatus, the dictator of Rome who, as soon as a crisis was resolved, went back to farming his fields. This Napoleon never did (despite a short period of exile spent planting chestnut trees on Elba) – he hung on to his throne too long, and therefore took away the lustre of his great achievements.

By 1815, almost everyone in France except Napoleon was exhausted by his war effort. Since the Revolution, about 1.4 million Frenchmen had died in battle.* In total, around 30 per cent of French males born between 1790 and 1795 were killed or wounded in uniform.

This is why anti-Bonapartists insist that Napoleon – not France – lost Waterloo. If he had won the battle, they say, the allies would have continued attacking, whereas his defeat ushered in a period of fifty-five years of relative peace in Europe – which only ended when Napoleon's nephew provoked Prussia in 1870. France then got rid of the last Bonaparte emperor, and enjoyed forty-three more years of European peace until World War One. All in all, they would say, Waterloo was the first step in 'curing' the Bonaparte problem that would otherwise have dogged France throughout the nineteenth century.

Nevertheless – a Bonapartist would argue – even statements like that place Napoleon at the heart of French history, as the catalyst for everything that succeeded his reign.

---

* Compared to 'only' 300,000 British men killed during the Napoleonic Wars. But then the French would argue that this was because Britain was paying foreign mercenaries to do its fighting – which was true. Around a million soldiers from the other allied countries also died.

II

It has not always been easy to voice anti-Bonapartist views in France. A telling example is Pierre Larousse's fifteen-volume encyclopedia, *Le Grand Dictionnaire Universel*, completed in 1876. It contains two separate definitions of Napoleon: under 'Bonaparte', in volume two which was first published in 1867, he is 'the greatest, most glorious, most striking name in history . . . a name that is easy to remember, simple, unified, military, with hard, short, dry consonants, a name that was unknown before him, but which was to engrave itself in the memory of all who heard it'. It reads like an advert for a French perfume.

However, at the entry for 'Napoléon 1er', in a volume published in 1874, there is an editor's note explaining that seven years earlier the dictionary had been forced to praise Napoleon 'for fear of compromising our publication'. The former Emperor is then defined as 'a man who was the cruellest enemy of freedom . . . a political and military dictator, an imitator of the Caesars'.

The explanation for this apparent schizophrenia is that the early volumes were published while Napoléon III, Bonaparte's nephew, was in power, the later ones just after his fall.

But the most interesting thing about all this is that in 2014, in a special Napoleonic edition of the French magazine *L'Histoire*, an article about the *Grand Dictionnaire*'s differing definitions failed to mention the time gap between the two volumes of the dictionary. It described the contrasting opinions as a sign that France has never been able to make up its mind about Napoleon.* In fact, though, the French have always divided themselves into two factions – *pour* and *contre* Napoleon. The thing is that bitterly negative opinions, like the definition of him as 'the cruellest enemy of freedom', have become much rarer since he and his nephew were ousted from power and their tyrannical tendencies stopped causing resentment. Now that the French can say what they like about Napoleon, it is simply the Bonapartists who are much more vocal.

III

Even though in 1815 France had ousted Napoleon for the second time in two years, with many French people calling for his head and the returning royalist aristocracy hungry for revenge against almost everything that had happened in France for the previous twenty-five years, post-Napoleonic France remained a surprisingly Napoleonic place – the key difference being that Napoleon himself was no longer there to force the French to obey *all* his rules and keep *all* his institutions.

Naturally, there were also sweeping political changes. During his first short reign from 1814 to early 1815, Louis XVIII had signed (albeit with the allies holding the pen) his so-called 'Charte constitutionelle', which ushered in some major anti-Bonapartist reforms. These were reintroduced

---

* When I wrote to the magazine pointing out this omission, I was of course ignored. A mere *Anglais* does not contradict a French history magazine, especially to point out uncomfortable truths.

after Waterloo. The Charte guaranteed the freedom of the press, freedom of religion, and opened up careers such as the law and medicine to poor but talented citizens. It also confirmed the property deeds of everyone who had bought land and property from dispossessed aristocrats and the royal family.

Astonishingly, Louis XVIII allowed the newly created Napoleonic aristocracy to keep its noble titles – though it is doubtful whether the average French citizen found having two aristocracies better than one. After all, a double layer of *crème de la crème* makes even the sweetest dessert taste sickly.

Louis XVIII stopped short of handing total power back to the aristos, however. Even he knew that they were incapable of ruling the country. The Charte therefore installed the new elite that still governs France – the technocrats, who were largely a product of the Napoleonic system, and who were now freed of subservience to either an emperor or a king.

At the same time as the restored monarchy was introducing a measure of British-style parliamentary democracy to France, there was also strong pressure from Britain to adopt its economic model. As we saw in Chapter 4, however, this met with a decisive French 'Merde!'. Turning its back on the free market, in 1815 France adopted its own strategy, a combination of Napoleonic patriotism and new freedom: Louis Becquey, who was given the grand new title of Directeur Général de l'Agriculture, du Commerce et des Arts et Manufactures, defined the strategy as 'liberté au-dedans, protectionnisme au-dehors' – 'freedom within, protectionism outside'. It is a technique that the French still use today, one that makes the European Union (and especially the Brits) howl with outrage every time France blocks the sale of a big French company to a foreign multi-national, or uses government subsidies to prop up its ailing industries, often in defiance of EU law.

So, after Waterloo, as Britain steamed ahead with the Industrial Revolution, flooding the world with its cheap cotton and metal products, and the spices, tea and sugar from its colonies, rather as China is doing now with its plastics, France did not try to follow suit (not that it had the money or the energy to do so).

Instead, it haughtily disapproved. The French politician Adolphe Blanqui – a royalist – visited England in 1823 and compared the factories of Wolverhampton to the fires of Mount Etna. He understood, he wrote in a book about his travels, how this small island had toppled Napoleon's 'great empire' (even a royalist could be nostalgic about France's recent glories): it was thanks to these factories that 'had forged the thunder sent against my homeland', meaning the hundreds of thousands of muskets and millions of bullets and cannonballs that had ripped France's armies to shreds. This English industrial might had become a plague, Blanqui declared, blanketing everything with black dust and 'forcing the English to cover the sea with their ships' so that they could export all their products.

It is a view that survives in France today: many French people still harbour Blanqui's distaste for unashamed capitalism, as well as a suspicion that bosses are evil slave-drivers, building themselves mansions in the country while the workers choke on poisonous fumes. Despite the huge international success of French entrepreneurs like the Renault brothers, Armand Peugeot and Paul Ricard, generating colossal profits has come to be thought of by many ordinary French people as a crass, 'Anglo-Saxon' character fault. Anyone in France who makes too much filthy lucre is seen as not really French.

The French can argue that it was actually an advantage to have been left behind (initially at least) by the Industrial Revolution. After 1815, France was forced to become self-sufficient, and it huddled down over its needles, its cheese-making machines and wine presses, making the most of the new post-Napoleonic peace by concentrating on its typically French crafts. And before long, rich British businesspeople were rushing to Paris to shop at the city's small, exclusive boutiques, buying lace, gloves, hats and silk garments, as well as fanning out into the countryside to buy wine and fine food direct from the farmers.

Free of Napoleon's trade barriers, the French were quickly able to enslave the British by selling them all the sophisticated things English factories were incapable of making. France's luxury industry – its greatest export today – was born out of the unique post-Waterloo economic conditions. Triumph in the battle for chic belongs to France.

Bonapartists often talk about the French people feeling 'orphaned' or left unprotected in 1815. A Napoleonic veteran, the former General Baron Thiebault, put it nicely in his memoirs, saying that 'With Napoleon gone, France was like a ship without sails or a compass, a plaything for the storm.' But in fact, the economic transition seems to have been much smoother. It was less a case of France losing its *pater familias* than emerging from childhood. Papa had retired from the family business – admittedly, not altogether willingly – and left the next generation free to run things as they wanted, in a more open, efficient way, undisturbed by war. As Victor Hugo put it in *Les Misérables*, 'the disappearance of the great man was necessary to usher in the great century'.

IV

The fall of Napoleon also ushered in a new period of cultural freedom in France, rather in the way that the end of Cromwell's puritan regime did in England.

Even if Napoleon had inspired foreign artists like Beethoven, Byron and Hegel while he was in power, at home he had overseen a period of cultural austerity. As a general, Napoleon had spent a lot of his campaign time looting foreign museums of their treasures, but as Emperor he had been fonder of the beauty of a well-expressed regulation. His only real artistic creativity was directed towards portraits of himself in heroic mode, grandiose self-aggrandising monuments, uniforms and propaganda. Under Napoleon, theatres were unable to decide their own programmes, and the anti-elitist satire that had grown out of the Revolution was well and truly stifled. Art had to be officially sanctioned.

On 29 November 1803, Napoleon wrote a letter to his

Minister of the Interior, Jean-Antoine Chaptal, saying: 'I desire you to commission . . . a song about the invasion of England . . . I know that several relevant plays have been put on; a selection should be made, so that they can be performed in Parisian theatres, and especially in the camps at Boulogne and Bruges, and wherever the army is stationed.' It is easy to imagine his soldiers' joy when showtime was announced, and instead of actresses reciting lewd poems, they got hymns and plays about attacking Kent.

To get an idea of Napoleon's view of culture, one only has to look at the regime he devised for the management of France's national theatre, the Comédie Française. In 1812, while in Moscow, he took time out from chasing the Czar to dictate a decree that turned French actors into a sort of army.

The Comédie Française, he ordered, would be 'placed under the surveillance and direction of the Superintendent of our theatre'. (By 'our', of course, Napoleon was referring to himself.) 'An Imperial Commissioner, named by us, will be responsible for transmitting the Superintendent's orders to the actors.' Actors had to sign up for twenty years, and obey strict rules of behaviour – they could be excused from performing if they were declared officially sick, but if seen out walking in the street or going to see a show while on the sick list, they would be fined.

There was little room for art or inspiration in all this – tragic actors were forbidden to play comedy, and roles were attributed according to seniority rather than talent. Only plays approved unanimously by nine committee members (named by the state) could be performed. Napoleon's list of rules ends chillingly: 'Our Ministers of the interior, of police, of finance and the Superintendent of our theatre are all given responsibility for the execution of the present decree.'

After Napoleon's exit from the world stage, the Comédie Française embraced the change of political regime, and began to choose for itself the plays it could produce. This seems to have been enough to satisfy the actors, because they didn't alter anything else in Napoleon's rules, which still govern the Comédie Française today. Performers sign up as *pension-naires* (apprentices) for a year, before being elected *sociétaires* (members), and their nomination has to be confirmed by the Ministry of Culture. Yet again, Bonapartists can claim a lasting victory for Napoleon's administrative skills.

And the new freedom did not mean that the Comédie suddenly started to honour France's new friends, the English, by programming a Shakespeare season. The bard was still considered much too anarchic for classical French tastes, and in 1822, a year after Napoleon's death, when a brave Frenchman tried to produce a performance of *Othello*, it was met with a barrage of eggs, fruit and cries of 'down with Shakespeare, he is the lieutenant of Wellington' – proving that the audience had not read the programme notes about the author not being a soldier.* To make matters worse, by this time many French people had begun to pronounce

* Unless the French crowd misunderstood Othello's line in Act Two, 'The purchase made, the fruits are to ensue', and thought it was a call for audience participation.

Wellington's name as 'Vilain-jeton', as Napoleon's soldiers had done. Literally, this means 'ugly fake coin', probably an allusion to a French term for 'hypocrite' – *faux jeton*.

But by bombarding the stage and insulting an English general, at least the French were taking advantage of their political liberty. And the rest of French culture also began to express itself more freely after Waterloo.

Freedom of the press spawned freedom of the written word in general, and the book trade began to expand. In 1813, 3,749 books had been published in France; by 1825 the figure was 7,605. Writers like Honoré de Balzac and Victor Hugo were free to talk about everyday life, poverty and the realities of war. Though as we saw in Chapter 7, Bonapartists can claim some credit for this literary renaissance, too, because much of the subject matter was inspired by nostalgia for France's former 'glory' under Napoleon.

The new spirit of expressiveness spread to music, too. Romanticism finally ousted classicism in France, prompting Liszt and Chopin to come and perform. Rossini became director of Paris's Théâtre Italien, and light-hearted entertainment thrived, so that by the 1840s the German-born composer Jacques Offenbach was in Paris writing the catchy melodies that would give birth to Vaudeville. The French frivolity that would later inspire the Belle Epoque was born in the heady peacetime post-Waterloo.*

It could also be argued that France's most memorable

---

* For more details about fun and frivolity in Parisian theatre, see my book *Dirty Bertie: An English King Made in France*.

contribution to world culture in the nineteenth century came about because of the fall of Napoleon. While he was in power, official painting was limited to glorifying the Emperor, his regime and its military heroes. The more a portrait looked like something looted from ancient Greece, the better. Things didn't change very quickly, and even in the 1850s, Paris's artistic establishment was staid enough to reject paintings by Edouard Manet that were considered not heroic enough. But soon, inspired by painters like Camille Corot and Gustave Courbet, a new generation of artists were freeing up their palettes, slapping on the colour, and painting portraits of simple peasants, waitresses and workers instead of emperors and generals. Impressionism was blossoming.

And where were the new artists doing this (with apologies for the French-style rhetorical question)? Mainly on the fringes of Paris, which, unlike London, was not expanding massively under the impetus of the Industrial Revolution. Even as late as the 1860s Montmartre was still a village, with peasants, fields and vineyards, less than 3 kilometres from the centre of Paris. Painters trained in the art schools and studios of the capital only had to wander a short way up the hill to find rustic inspiration and cheap accommodation, free of the smog that would have blackened their brushes if they had tried the same thing in London. Just a few kilometres further out, in the unchanging French countryside, they could paint peaceful sunlit picnics, *bourgeois* pretending to be peasants, and women wearing floaty dresses and looking quintessentially French. And when the Impressionists turned to urban life, they painted a few cityscapes and puffing trains, but most of all they immortalised *Parisiennes* sporting the chic hand-made dresses, hats and parasols that were being turned out in the city's workshops.

All in all, it can be argued that France's place in art history was founded on the economic tranquillity that reigned in the country after Waterloo and the fall of Napoleon. Again, the French are the winners.

V

The conclusion, then, is clear. The Brits and the Germans might think that they won the great battle on 18 June 1815, but if you take a step back and examine history through French eyes – Bonapartist or not – things look very different.

Like Cambronne's last square of defiant *Gardes*, the French are surrounded by hostile (mainly British) historians reminding them that Waterloo was lost, and that the day ended with everyone in a French uniform – including the most famous uniform of them all – running for their lives. But either they will contradict you, or they don't care.

Even if you can get a French person to admit that Napoleon was defeated at Waterloo – which will probably involve your conceding that he won more battles than he lost, that he had bad luck with the weather, and that his piles were playing up on that fateful June day – you will be forced to agree that Napoleon is a far more famous and recognisable icon today than either Wellington or Blücher. Who has won the battle for history? the French person will ask; and, being French, he or she will also provide the answer: *c'est Napoléon*.

Furthermore, this French person will argue that even if Napoleon was defeated on 18 June 1815, France as a nation emerged a winner, because it was allowed to keep everything that was useful about Bonapartism, and build on those foundations to become a well-organised bureaucratic republic, the birthplace of Impressionism and the world capital of the luxury industry – not to mention making a fortune out of Napoleonic tourism and selling Napoleonic memorabilia.

And if you haven't given up arguing yet, and continue to contradict your French debating partner, he or she will simply pull one decisive trick out of Napoleon's million-euro black hat: all discussion will be ended with the triumphant word that France first learned how to use to its full effect at Waterloo – *merde*.

In short, there was one critical thing that Wellington and Blücher didn't know when they took on the French at Waterloo, one unavoidable fact that we today are forced to acknowledge: when you're up against Napoleon, you just can't win.

EPILOGUE

As I finish writing this book, France is in a mood of crushing pessimism. Most of this is caused by day-to-day economic gloom and the fear of terrorist attacks, but a fair proportion is more deeply rooted in a painful combination of wounded pride and vicious self-criticism. With its declining influence in world affairs, the replacement of French by English as a global language, as well as its current economic problems, France seems to be more aware than ever that it has frittered away all the *gloire* that Napoleon earned for it 200 years ago.

This negativity is exactly the kind of mood that Napoleon could have cured – with a quick war to annex Luxembourg, perhaps – and one that is alleviated today by regular bouts of Napoleonic nostalgia.

One of these therapy sessions we have already heard about – the November 2014 auction in the 'imperial town' of Fontainebleau of Napoleonic memorabilia at which one of the Emperor's hats was sold for 1.8 million euros. During the sale, France's core psychological problems were highlighted by two key slips of the tongue.

First, while talking about a historian who had researched the provenance of Napoleon's possessions in the sale, one of the auctioneers committed a hugely revealing Freudian slip. Instead of 'un historien', he called the man 'un hystérien', thereby inventing a piercingly accurate description of Napoleon's most nostalgic admirers.

A second, and even more telling, mistake came when the main auctioneer was reciting Edmond Rostand's lines of poetry about Napoleon's hat. As I pointed out in Chapter 8, he completely fluffed the last two lines. But most revealingly of all, he omitted one vital word. Rostand wrote that the sound to be heard inside Napoleon's shell-like hat was that of 'une grande nation' on the march – but the auctioneer forgot to say 'grande'. Subconsciously, while surrounded by the relics of Napoleon's legendary career, he was admitting that modern France just isn't 'great' any more.

This is why French people today seem to feel that they need Napoleon. Or at least *a* Napoleon. The politicians try to emulate him, but they all fall absurdly short (which is not a height-related pun). When France's Prime Minister, Manuel Valls, travelled to London in October 2014, he was ostensibly coming to convince both the City of London and French tax exiles that his Socialist regime was not hostile to business; but it soon became clear that his was a different mission, and one that probably set Napoleon's *cendres* spinning in his sarcophagus.

Monsieur Valls told his audience of businesspeople (in

French of course), 'Every day I read your press, I hear and I see what is being said about France. Too often in some of your newspapers I see bias, prejudices and attacks.' Yes, in reality he had come to London to complain about *le French-bashing*, a piece of English vocabulary that is so hurtful to the French national psyche that they have actually adopted it into their language.

In short, in 2014 a French Prime Minister crossed the Channel to complain to *les Anglais* that they were saying nasty things about France. Two centuries earlier, Napoleon and all his troops, right up to the highest-ranked marshals, had stood impassively on the battlefield as British cannonballs were fired at their heads, and now a French politician was whinging about a few insults? At the very least he could have unleashed a decent retort of 'Merde!' instead of pleading for the barrage of French-bashing to stop. It was a defeat 200 times more humiliating than Waterloo (if, of course, Waterloo was a defeat, etc., etc.).

In the face of such defeatism among their political leaders, it is no wonder that the French are gearing up for several years of Napoleonic celebration. It seems to be the only way to restore a mood of national pride.

The biggest of a series of Napoleon-themed projects in the offing is the proposed Parc Napoléon at Montereau, 80 kilometres from Paris, the site of one of Napoleon's final victories in 1814. This 200-million-euro theme park, due to be completed by 2020, is the brainchild of the town's MP. It aims to attract 400,000 visitors in the first year, rising to two million in year ten, and will apparently include hotels, a conference centre and of course a battlefield for regular Napoleonic re-enactments (which, given the location, will no doubt all result in French victories). The project has already attracted promises of funding from the French state as well as investment from China and the Emirates, with plenty more money in the pipeline, we are told. Such far-reaching, and expensive, recognition is the Bonapartists' dream, even if a theme park does seem to place Napoleon at the same cultural level as Mickey Mouse.

Meanwhile, thousands of kilometres away in the South Atlantic, there is a similar plan to turn the island of Saint Helena into a kind of exiled Parc Napoléon. France owns 17 hectares of land on the British island. These French properties cover three locations: The Briars (the garden pavilion where Napoleon spent his first few weeks of exile on the island in 1815), the land around Napoleon's last residence at Longwood, and his original grave – his body was of course later repatriated to France. Longwood and the grave site were bought for the French nation by Emperor Napoléon III in 1857, while The Briars was gifted to France in 1959 by the English family that had owned it since 1815. The original grave, by the way, was just a square slab of stone on a lawn, but has since been fenced off to prevent Bonapartists prostrating themselves and sobbing loud enough to startle the seagulls.

Recently, Longwood has been renovated by the French at a cost of some 2.3 million euros, 1.5 million of which came from 2,500 private and corporate donors, and the rest from the French state. This sizeable sum did not cover the restoration of the furniture, and over thirty pieces were sent back to France's national workshops to be refurbished before their return to Longwood.

This costly renovation of Napoleon's prison island is part of a Bonapartist masterplan, starting with a *grande inauguration* of the new-look Longwood on 15 October 2015 (the bicentenary of Napoleon's arrival on Saint Helena), followed by a series of visits throughout 2016 by French groups, and a grand tour of the island by the International Napoleonic Society in 2017, with the excitement coming to a climax on the 200th anniversary of Napoleon's death on 5 May 2021.

Meanwhile, there has been some harsh French criticism of the Brits for not playing their part in this bonanza of Napoleonic activity on Saint Helena. In 2014 *L'Histoire* magazine reproached the islanders for their 'insufficient hospitality: just 40-odd hotel rooms and six restaurants, all of poor standard'. Usually, of course, Bonapartists criticise *les Anglais* for their rampant commercialism, but when it comes to glorifying Napoleon, commercialism is clearly acceptable.

The French memorial ceremony on Saint Helena in May 2021 is going to be a major event. No doubt French politicians will be flocking to pay their respects in front of the cameras, praying that they can scoop up a few crumbs of Napoleonic *gloire* for themselves. And we can be sure that the island will be echoing to the Bonapartists' cries of 'Vive l'Empereur!' even as they commemorate his death.

By then, a five-star Hotel Napoleon, a Longwood Luncheonette and a Bonaparte Brasserie had better be ready on Saint Helena, or there will be some serious *Anglais*-bashing on the menu. Because this will be the modern Bonapartists' great moment, the focus of all their energy for at least the past century. They are currently bringing Napoleonic nostalgia to a climax, whipping re-enactors and auction-goers to new heights of hysteria, spreading the Bonaparte gospel as far as Asia, and attracting investors for his theme park from all over the world. Napoleon is as recognisable an icon today as he ever was, and is well on his way to being even bigger than Mickey Mouse. So the threat is very real: if *les Anglais* don't show enough respect to *l'Empereur* on the bicentenary of his entry into immortality, his worshippers might just annex the whole island and declare it the capital of a new Napoleonic empire . . .

APPENDIX 1

Napoleon's verbal salvoes

Rather like a French Shakespeare, Napoleon spent much of his life producing quotable quotes – the difference between the two men being that most of Napoleon's were about himself.

Here are a few Napoleonic sayings, not used elsewhere in the book, that give an insight into the *Empereur*'s inner workings.

'This battle [Waterloo] was against the interests of his [Wellington's] nation and the allies' overall war plan; it violated all the rules of war . . . It was not in England's interests . . . to expose itself so frivolously to a murderous struggle that could have cost it its only army and its purest blood.'

'You English will weep that you won Waterloo! In the end,

posterity, well-informed people, genuine statesmen and genuinely good men will bitterly regret that I did not succeed in all my undertakings.'

'Europe will soon be weeping over the loss of balance to which my French empire was absolutely necessary. It is in great danger. At any moment, it may be flooded with Cossacks and Tartars.'

'Every nation is the same. When you give them golden chains, they don't dislike servitude.'

'Good politics is making people believe that they are free.'

'What I am striving for is greatness. Great things are always beautiful.'

'Coldness is the best quality for a man who is destined to command.'

'The cannon killed feudalism. Ink will kill modern society.'

'I am more frightened of three newspapers than of 100,000 bayonets.'

'Peace is a meaningless word. What we want is glorious peace.'

'Trade brings men together, everything that brings men

together binds them, so trade is essentially harmful to authority.'

'For one woman who inspires us to do good, there are a hundred who make us behave like idiots.'

'There is one thing that isn't French – that a woman can do what she wants.'

'Our ridiculous failing as a country is that the greatest enemy of our success and our glory is ourselves.'

'It is in the French character to exaggerate, to complain and to distort everything when one is unhappy.'

'You can stop when you are on the way up, but not on the way down.'

'Death is nothing, but to die beaten and without glory is to die every day.'

APPENDIX 2

Contemporary views of Waterloo

Part of Napoleon's speech to his soldiers on 15 June 1815, reminding them of the good old days (the text was printed and widely distributed in Belgium before the battle):

> Soldiers! These same Prussians who are so arrogant today were three to one against you at Jena [in Germany, in 1806], six to one at Montmirail [in France, in 1814].
>
> Those among you who were prisoners in England can tell their comrades what frightful torments they suffered on board the English hulks.
>
> The Saxons, Belgians, Hanoverians, and the soldiers of the Rhine Confederation are sad to be forced to serve the cause of princes who are enemies of justice and people's rights. They know that this coalition is insatiable. After devouring twelve million Italians, a million Saxons and six million Belgians, it will devour all the smaller states of Germany.

Madmen! One moment of prosperity has blinded them. The oppression and humiliation of the French people is beyond their capability. If they enter into France it will be to find a grave there!

Soldiers, we have forced marches to make, battles to fight, dangers to face; but with steadfastness, victory will be ours. The rights, the honour and the happiness of our homeland will be won back.

Excerpts from William Makepeace Thackeray's novel *Vanity Fair* (published in 1847–8), showing how rumours of what was going on in Waterloo reached Brussels:

All that day from morning until past sunset, the cannon never ceased to roar. It was dark when the cannonading stopped all of a sudden. All of us have read of what occurred during that interval. The tale is in every Englishman's mouth; and you and I, who were children when the great battle was won and lost, are never tired of hearing and recounting the history of that famous action. Its remembrance rankles still in the bosoms of millions of the countrymen of those brave men who lost the day. They pant for an opportunity of revenging that humiliation; and if a contest, ending in a victory on their part, should ensue, elating them in their turn, and leaving its cursed legacy of hatred and rage behind to us, there is no end to the so-called glory and shame, and to the alternations of successful and unsuccessful murder, in which two high-spirited nations might engage. Centuries hence, we

Frenchmen and Englishmen might be boasting and killing each other still.

[. . .]

Several times during the forenoon Mr. Jos's [servant] Isidor went from his lodgings into the town, and to the gates of the hotels and lodging-houses round about the Parc, where the English were congregated, and there mingled with other valets, couriers, and lackeys, gathered such news as was abroad, and brought back bulletins for his master's information. Almost all these gentlemen were in heart partisans of the Emperor, and had their opinions about the speedy end of the campaign. [. . .] It was agreed on all hands that Prussians and British would never return except as prisoners in the rear of the conquering army.

These opinions in the course of the day were brought to operate upon Mr. Sedley. He was told that the Duke of Wellington had gone to try and rally his army, the advance of which had been utterly crushed the night before.

"Crushed, psha!" said Jos, whose heart was pretty stout at breakfast-time. "The Duke has gone to beat the Emperor as he has beaten all his generals before."

"His papers are burned, his effects are removed, and his quarters are being got ready for the Duke of Dalmatia," Jos's informant replied. "I had it from his own maitre d'hotel. Milor Duc de Richemont's people are packing up everything. His Grace has fled already, and the Duchess is only waiting to see the plate packed to join the King of France at Ostend."

"The King of France is at Ghent, fellow," replied Jos, affecting incredulity.

"He fled last night to Bruges, and embarks today from Ostend. The Duc de Berri [Louis XVIII's nephew] is taken prisoner. Those who wish to be safe had better go soon, for the dykes will be opened to-morrow, and who can fly when the whole country is under water?"

"Nonsense, sir, we are three to one, sir, against any force Boney can bring into the field," Mr. Sedley objected; "the Austrians and the Russians are on their march. He must, he shall be crushed," Jos said, slapping his hand on the table.

"The Prussians were three to one at Jena, and he took their army and kingdom in a week. They were six to one at Montmirail, and he scattered them like sheep. The Austrian army is coming, but with the Empress and the King of Rome [Napoleon's wife and son] at its head; and the Russians, bah! the Russians will withdraw. No quarter is to be given to the English, on account of their cruelty to our braves on board the infamous pontoons. Look here, here it is in black and white. Here's the proclamation of his Majesty the Emperor and King," said the now declared partisan of Napoleon, and taking the document from his pocket, Isidor sternly thrust it into his master's face, and already looked upon the frogged coat and valuables as his own spoil.

Jos was, if not seriously alarmed as yet, at least considerably disturbed in mind.

Napoleon's reaction after Waterloo

After the defeat, denial set in straight away. Here are some excerpts from Napoleon's official report, the *Bulletin de*

l'Armée, written on 20 June, as he was fleeing towards Paris.
Note that he calls Waterloo 'the Battle of Mont-Saint-Jean'.

He begins with some triumphalism over his success at
Ligny:

At 7.30, we had captured forty cannons, many carriages,
flags and prisoners, and the enemy was looking to save itself
in hasty retreat. At ten o'clock, the battle was over, and we
were masters of the battlefield.

General Lützow had been captured. Prisoners assured
us that Fieldmarshal Blücher had been wounded. The elite
of the Prussian army had been destroyed. Its losses cannot
have been less than 15,000; ours were only 3,000 killed or
wounded.

[. . .]

At 3 p.m. [on 18 June], the Emperor [Napoleon often
referred to himself in his reports in the third person] decided
to attack via the village of Mont-Saint-Jean, and thereby
win a decisive victory; but thanks to an impatience that is
very common in our military annals, and which has so often
proved fatal to us, the reserve cavalry, seeing the English
retreat to shelter from our artillery, which had caused them
considerable damage, moved to the ridge at Mont-Saint-Jean
and charged the infantry. This movement, if it had been
executed at the right time, and supported, would have won
the day, but it was carried out in isolation and, before matters
came to a close on the right, became fatal.

[. . .]

There, for three hours, several charges overran English

squares and won us six infantry flags, but these gains were outweighed by the losses incurred by our cavalry from grapeshot and musket volleys.

[Even so, the French attacks began to take effect and, in mid-afternoon . . .]

The battle was won; we were occupying all the positions that the enemy had occupied at the start of the battle; because our cavalry had been engaged too soon and wrongly, we could not hope for a more decisive victory, but Marshal Grouchy, having assessed the movement of the Prussian army, was pursuing them, thereby assuring us of a great victory the following day. After eight hours of firing and infantry and cavalry charges, the whole army was able to look with satisfaction upon a battle won and the battlefield in our possession.

[Then, however, something inexplicable happened. The advance of the *Moyenne Garde* was met with an unexpected attack from the flank and . . .]

The nearby regiments, who saw a few soldiers of the *Garde* retreating, thought that they were from the *Vieille Garde*, and weakened: shouts of 'all is lost, the *Garde* has been pushed back!' were heard. Some soldiers claim that there were agitators present, who shouted 'every man for himself!' Whether this is true or not, panic and terror instantly spread across the battlefield. Men fled in total disorder along our communication lines. Soldiers, artillery-men, ammunition carriers were trying to advance; even the *Vieille Garde*, who were in reserve, were swept away.

In an instant, the army was a confused mass, all its

elements mixed up, and it was impossible to re-form a fighting force. Darkness prevented us from rallying the troops and showing them that they were mistaken. In this way, a completed battle plan, a day's accomplishments, mistakes repaired, greater success ensured for the following day – all were lost in one moment of panic. Even the squadrons at the Emperor's side were jostled and disorganised by the tumultuous rush, and could do nothing but follow the flood. [. . .] We know what the bravest army in the world becomes when it is confused and loses its organisation.

[. . .]

The enemy's losses must have been great, to judge by the flags that we captured and the retreats they were forced to make [. . .] The artillery, as usual, covered itself in glory. Thus ended the Battle of Mont-Saint-Jean, glorious for the French army, and yet so disastrous.

Wellington's account

Some excerpts from Wellington's report, written the day after the battle and published in *The Times* and the *London Gazette Extraordinary* on Thursday, 22 June 1815.

The report is addressed to Britain's Secretary for War, Earl Bathurst, and gives the view of events that Wellington had thus far managed to piece together from his own experiences and those of his officers. It was obviously written before anyone had decided what exactly to call the battle, though Wellington was staying in the nearest small town to the battlefield and therefore headed his report 'Waterloo, June 19th 1815'.

This excerpt retains Wellington's own spellings, including the British refusal to spell Napoleon's surname the way he wanted.

He begins with an account of the fighting on the days leading up to 18 June, and then moves on to what we now call Waterloo:

[. . .] The enemy collected his army, with the exception of the third corps, which had been sent to observe Marshal Blucher, on a range of heights to our front, in the course of the night of the 17th and yesterday morning: and at about ten o'clock he commenced a furious attack upon our post at Hougoumont [. . .] I am happy to add, that it was maintained throughout the day with the utmost gallantry by these brave troops, notwithstanding the repeated efforts of large bodies of the enemy to obtain possession of it.

This attack upon the right of our centre was accompanied by a very heavy cannonade upon our whole line, which was destined to support the repeated attacks of cavalry and infantry occasionally mixed, but some times separate, which were made upon it. In one of these the enemy carried the farm house of La Haye Sainte, as the detachment of the light battalion of the legion which occupied it had expended all its ammunition [. . .]

The enemy repeatedly charged our infantry with his cavalry, but these attacks were uniformly unsuccessful, and they afforded opportunities to our cavalry to charge, in one of which Lord E. Somerset's brigade, consisting of the life guards, royal horse guards, and first dragoon guards, highly distinguished themselves, as did that of Major General Sir W. Ponsonby, having taken many prisoners and an eagle.

These attacks were repeated until about seven in the evening, when the enemy made a desperate effort with the cavalry and infantry, supported by the fire of artillery, to force our left centre near the farm of La Haye Sainte, which after a severe contest was defeated, and having observed that the troops retired from this attack in great confusion, and that the marc[h] of General Bulow's corps by Euschermont upon Planchernerte and la Belle alliance, had begun to take effect, and as I could perceive the fire of his cannon, and as Marshal Prince Blucher had joined in person, with a corps of his army to the left of our line by Ohaim, I determined to attack the enemy, and immediately advanced the whole line of infantry, supported by the cavalry and artillery. The attack succeeded in every point; the enemy was forced from his position on the heights, and fled in the utmost confusion, leaving behind him, as far as I could judge, one hundred and fifty pieces of cannon, with their ammunition, which fell into our hands. I continued the pursuit till long after dark, and then discontinued it only on account of the fatigue of our troops, and because I found myself on the same road with Marshal Blucher, who assured me of his intention to pursue the enemy throughout the night; he had sent me word this morning that he had taken sixty pieces of cannon belonging to the Imperial Guard, and several carriages, baggage, &c, belonging to Buonaparte, in Genappe [. . .]

Your Lordship will observe, that such a desperate action could not be fought, and such advantages could not be gained, without great loss; and I am sorry to add, that ours has been immense.

[. . .]

It gives me the greatest satisfaction to assure your Lordship, that the army never, upon any occasion, conducted itself better [. . .] and here is no Officer or description of troops that did not behave well.

[. . .]

I should not do justice to my feelings or to Marshal Blucher and the Prussian army, if I do not attribute the successful result of this arduous day, to the cordial and timely assistance I received from them.

The operation of General Bulow, upon the enemy's flank, was a most decisive one; and even if I had not found myself in a position to make the attack, which produced the final result, it would have forced the enemy to retire, if his attacks should have failed, and would have prevented him from taking advantage of them, if they should unfortunately have succeeded.

I send, with this despatch, two eagles, taken by the troops in action, which Major Percy will have the honour of laying at the feet of his Royal Highness.

I beg leave to recommend him to your Lordship's protection. I have the honour, &c,

Wellington.

Napoleon's farewell messages

On 22 June 1815, a deputation of French MPs came to express their support for Napoleon (while 'congratulating' him on the wisdom of his decision to abdicate for the second time). He told them:

I thank you for the sentiments that you have expressed towards me; I desire that my abdication should bring happiness to France, but I doubt that it will; it leaves the state without a head, without political existence. The time wasted overturning the monarchy could have been used to ensure that France was in a fit state to crush the enemy. I recommend that the House [of representatives] should reinforce the army promptly; whoever wants peace should prepare for war. Do not put this great nation at the mercy of foreigners. Beware of disappointed hopes. Whatever happens to me, I will always be happy if France is happy.

On 25 June, Napoleon dictated a farewell letter to his troops:

Soldiers, as I surrender to the necessity which forces me away from my brave French army, I take with me the happy certainty that it will perform the duties that the homeland asks of it, and thereby earn the praise that even our enemies cannot deny us.

Soldiers, I will follow your movements, even in my absence. I know each regiment, and I will recognise the courage that each of them has shown every time they win an advantage over the enemy. You and I have been slandered. Men who are unworthy of judging your efforts have interpreted your loyalty to me as excessive zeal, of which I was the only object. May your future successes show them that by obeying me you were above all serving our homeland, and that, if I have earned your affection, it is only because of my passionate love for France, our common motherland.

Soldiers, with just a little more effort, the coalition will be dissolved. Napoleon will know you by the blows that you strike. Save the honour and independence of the French people. Stay as I have known you for twenty years and you will be invincible.

Napoleon's letter was never published, or read out: his treacherous head of secret police Joseph Fouché found it, and hid it.

BIBLIOGRAPHY

There have to date been an estimated 80,000 books written about Napoleon, though that number is of course changing all the time. Apparently one new book or article gets published every week.

However, most history books quote the same basic sources, especially the accounts written by veterans of the battle. All the rest – including this book – is opinion and interpretation.

Here is a short list of the most useful, interesting, and (not always deliberately) amusing sources that I have read.

The French veterans' accounts are mostly available on the Bibliothèque Nationale's excellent website, gallica.fr.

The dates in brackets indicate the publication date of the edition consulted.

All quotations from French sources used in this book are my own translations. The same goes for the German. As for the lines from the Polish national anthem quoted in Chapter 8, I was forced to trust someone else.

Anonymous, *Relation fidèle et détaillée de la dernière campagne de Buonaparte, terminée par la bataille de Mont-Saint-Jean, dite de Waterloo ou de la Belle-Alliance, par un témoin oculaire* (1815)

Blanqui, Jérôme-Adolphe, *Voyage d'un jeune Français en Angleterre et en Ecosse pendant l'automne de 1823* (1824)

Chapuis, Colonel, *Notice sur le 85e de ligne pendant la campagne de 1815* (1838)

Charras, Jean-Baptiste-Adolphe, *Histoire de la Campagne de 1815 – Waterloo* (1857)

Coignet, Capitaine, *Les Cahiers 1799-1815* (1883)

Cronin, Vincent, *Napoleon Bonaparte: an Intimate Biography* (1971)

Damamme, Jean-Claude, *La Bataille de Waterloo* (1999)

Duthilt, Pierre-Charles, *Mémoires du Capitaine Duthilt* (1909)

Fleischmann, Hector, *Victor Hugo, Waterloo, Napoléon, documents recueillis* (1912)

Gallo, Max, *Napoléon, l'Immortel de Sainte-Hélène* (1997)

Home, George, *The Memoirs of an Aristocrat* (1838)

Houssaye, Henry, *Napoléon homme de guerre* (1904)

Hugo, Victor, 'L'Expiation' (poem from *Les Châtiments*, 1853)

—— *Les Misérables, Deuxième Partie, Livre 1* (1862)

Larreguy de Civrieux, Sylvain, *Souvenirs d'un cadet, 1812-1823* (1912)

Las Cases, Emmanuel de, *Le Mémorial de Sainte-Hélène* (1823)

Lemonnier-Delafosse, Marie Jean Baptiste, *Campagnes de 1810-1815 ou Souvenirs Militaires* (1850)

Macdonald, Etienne-Jacques-Joseph-Alexandre, *Souvenirs du Maréchal Macdonald, duc de Tarente* (1892)

Marq, François, *Descriptions des campagnes de guerre faites par moi* (1817)

Martin, Jacques-François, *Souvenirs d'un ex-officier, 1812–1815* (1867)

Mauduit, Hippolyte de, *Histoire des derniers jours de la Grande Armée, ou Souvenirs, documents et correspondance inédite de Napoléon en 1814 et 1815* (1854)

Mercer, General Cavalié, *Journal of the Waterloo Campaign, Kept throughout the Campaign of 1815* (1870)

Rogniat, *Considérations sur l'art de la guerre* (1816)

Scott, Sir Walter, *The Life of Napoleon Buonaparte, Emperor of the French* (1827)

Shelley, Frances, *The Diary of Frances Lady Shelley* (1912)

Thackeray, William Makepeace, *Vanity Fair* (1847–8)

Villepin, Dominique de, *Les Cent Jours ou l'Esprit du Sacrifice* (2001)

PICTURE PERMISSIONS

1. Napoleon on horseback, 1814. Mary Evans Picture Library
2. Napoleon Bonaparte by Ingres, 1806. Getty Images
3. Napoleon Bonaparte holding a soldier's ear. Mary Evans Picture Library
4. Napoleon's abdication speech, 1814. Getty Images
5. Napoleon, defeated. Mary Evans Picture Library
6. Napoleon's handiwork. Mary Evans Picture Library
7. Battle of Waterloo, 1815. Getty Images
8. Cambronne at the Battle of Waterloo, 1815. Getty Images
9. Marshal Michel Ney. Getty Images
10. Marshal General Nicolas Jean-de-Dieu Soult. Getty Images
11. Emmanuel de Grouchy. Getty Images
12. 'Sunken Lane', French retreat at Waterloo. Getty Images
13. Battle greeting of Blücher and Wellington. Getty Images

14. Napoleon sails into exile. Mary Evans Picture Library
15. Napoleon's remains arrive in Paris. Getty Images
16. Buffalo Bill's Wild West show. Mary Evans Picture Library.

Index

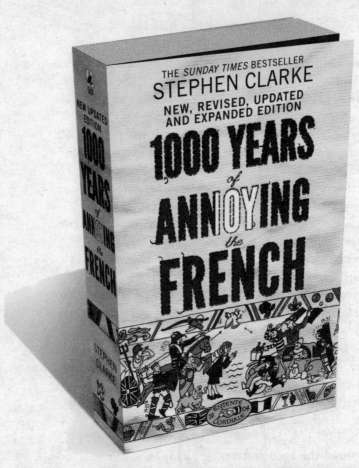

NEW FULLY REVISED, UPDATED AND EXPANDED EDITION

Ten centuries' worth of French historical 'facts' bite the dust as Stephen Clarke looks at what has really been going on since 1066 . . .

Featuring new annoyances — both historical and recent — inflicted on the French, including Napoleon's 'banned' chamber pot, Louis XIV's painful operation, Anglo-French jibes during the 2012 London Olympics, French niggles about William and Kate's royal wedding, and much more . . .

'Tremendously entertaining' *Sunday Times*

'Relentlessly and energetically rude' *Mail on Sunday*